R0061610937

01/2012

D1490706

The Half-Lived Life

ALSO BY JOHN LEE

The Half-Lived Life

*Overcoming Passivity and Rediscovering
Your Authentic Self*

JOHN LEE

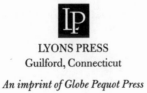

LYONS PRESS
Guilford, Connecticut

An imprint of Globe Pequot Press

In memory of Dan Jones

Lyons Press is an imprint of Globe Pequot Press.

Poem on p. 53: William Stafford, excerpt from "A Story That Could Be True" from *The Way It Is: New and Selected Poems.* Copyright © 1962, 1998 by William Stafford and the Estate of William Stafford. Reprinted with permission of The Permissions Company, Inc., on behalf of Graywolf Press, Minneapolis, Minnesota, www.graywolfpress.org.

Text design: Sheryl Kober
Layout artist: Melissa Evarts
Project editor: Kristen Mellitt

Library of Congress Cataloging-in-Publication Data is available on file.

ISBN 978-0-7627-7252-0

Printed in the United States of America

10 9 8 7 6 5 4 3 2 1

What is it you plan to do with your one wild and precious life?
—MARY OLIVER

Most people go to their graves with their music inside them.
—OLIVER WENDELL HOLMES

Contents

INTRODUCTION

YOUR AUTHENTIC LIFE AWAITS

Do not go where the path may lead. Go instead where there is no path and leave a trail.

—RALPH WALDO EMERSON

When does the search for an authentic life begin? Is it in middle age, or after retirement, or the minute you become a grandparent? For some it starts as early as their twenties, others their forties; for far too many it could be their sixties. When your quest begins is entirely up to you. But you'll know you're there when you suddenly realize that *it's your time.* You'll wake up and realize that each day is precious. You don't want to waste another minute surviving; you want to start thriving.

The next stage of your life should be characterized by one word— energy.

The next stage of your life should be characterized by one word—energy. It can be exciting, strange, wonderful, and a little bit scary. It will be even scarier if your second half looks and feels too much like the first. What you believe, what you think, and how you behave should be very different at fifty than at fifteen.

Sometimes a life event—good or bad—can suddenly hurl you into uncharted territory by forcing your hand and demanding a change of course or thought. Perhaps you were laid off from a job you thought would be there until retirement. Maybe you retired and realized you couldn't make ends meet. Or did you find yourself with an empty nest and wonder, *What now?*

Regardless of the motivating or mitigating factors that brought you to this stage, you want to move forward, but you may not know how.

The fact that you found this book was no accident. You're ready to move on to the next adventure, and this book will help you get there on your own terms.

Here are the promises I can make to you. If you take the tools, insights, information, and inspiration presented here in this book and practice them:

- You will get clarity on what you really want and come out of any residual passivity that may be impeding you from capturing your dream and turning it into reality.

- You will become fully engaged and alive.

- You will become compassionately assertive, able to say what you want and need.

- You will learn to love actively.

- You will come to trust your instincts, passions, and gut as well as the still, small voice that almost went completely silent.

- You will become an explorer in and an expert on your own and others' passivity.

- You will have enough information to conquer the passivity that limits you in the areas of relationships, work, family, friendship, love, and creativity.

Passivity, which is discussed in great detail later in this book, is the compulsion to pursue the opposite of what we say we want. Sounds crazy, doesn't it? And yet most of you will recognize your own and other people's passive tendencies in the pages of this book. The good news is: There's a lot you can do to overcome passivity and live a rich life that you can be genuinely excited about.

We have worn the disguise for so long, we actually think our false self is our true self.

Passivity can manifest as self-sabotage, settling for less, deferring dreams, or turning to denial or substitution. For example, you may have dreamed of becoming a dancer, but instead you became an accountant who works seventy hours a week and feels exhausted all the time. To the outside world you look like a "doer," but the truth is that you're hiding who you are under a mask.

Passivity is a true shape-shifter that can take different forms. It takes on so many different disguises that it not only confuses others but—after a while—even fools us. We have worn the disguise for so long, we actually think our false self is our true self. It is this passive false self that stifles and sometimes smothers truth, growth, passion, and creativity.

Over the last twenty-five years of my writing and teaching life, I have consistently explored and taught the things I needed to learn myself. My own undiagnosed and unaddressed passivity has been a silent saboteur that I unwittingly nurtured with the hope that no one would notice. And almost nobody did.

I exercised my passivity by being a workaholic and telling myself that I was doing it for the benefit of others. I spread myself so thin that there was almost nothing left at the end of the day for me or for my loved ones.

Until recently, it damaged my relationships, crippled communication with those I cared about, and infected my creative life like a plague that had no cure.

When I finally realized that passivity had been the cause of my dysfunctional thinking and behavior, I set out to get rid of it. However, the information available on passivity was not readily accessible, and the explanations were complicated. In my own journey to lead a fully lived life, I wrote this book for all of us who suffer from this problem, including myself.

To live more fully during the next part of our life, we must root out the passivity that corrodes human contact and makes a mockery out of the words *intimacy, love, compassion, passion,* and *purpose.*

For far too long psychologists, therapists, self-help writers, and the general public have been in the dark and therefore in denial about this demon that weakens our ability to handle depression, bad relationships, anxiety, and fear. It leads to underachievement, being passed over for promotions, and financial stagnation.

Do you want to live your life fully in charge of your destiny and unabashedly joyful? Then you have to learn to spot passivity wherever it rears its chameleon head and go against it with all the strength you can muster. If we engage in this battle for authenticity, we can live full lives that are characterized by energy, consciousness, compassion, and deep caring for one another, ourselves, and our planet. If we don't, we can sit in quiet desperation waiting for someone or something to rescue us from our passive malaise.

Until now only a handful of academic, neo-Freudians have been the ones discussing—in intellectual and clinical language—the passivity problem that plagues us as individuals and as a society. The few books that tackle this issue are difficult to read at best and impossible at worst. What you have in your hands is a translation of sorts from highbrow, intellectual probing to a down-to-earth explanation of the problem. My user-friendly language and approach avoid shaming, blaming, and demeaning anyone who is struggling with this issue

It is time to be who you really were meant to be and do what you were meant to do. so that you can make your own private pilgrimage through the mine/mind fields of passivity—guilt-free.

My last twenty years went by as if they were ten, and I suspect my next twenty will feel even faster. If your years feel as fleeting, you know that you don't have a lot of extra time to waste before releasing your unused life and energy.

It is time to be who you really were meant to be and do what you were meant to do. Now you can be the engaged, loving, successful, and creative person you have always believed and dreamed you could be. If you have often felt your glass is half empty in any area of life, this book can change all that.

It is important to note that the passivity I am discussing here in *The Half-Lived Life* is *not* to be confused with apathy, laziness, or procrastination. The passivity that is explained and explored here is what leaves many people feeling like they are giving up, defeated, settling, underachieving, or perpetually unsatisfied.

The Half-Lived Life provides solutions and ways out of this taxing state of mind, body, and spirit while increasing and enhancing your emotional intelligence quotient (EQ). This book—like my national workshops, trainings, and seminars—will take a holistic, proactive approach and weave together ideas and insights that are offered to us by psychologists, poets, and mythologists. It will use spiritual traditions, case histories, experiential exercises, and much more to explain a complex problem in a simple way.

Once you start digging your way out of the passive pit, you start reconnecting to your true self. I often refer to this reconnection as "remembering who you wanted to be." Most people remember a moment in their childhood, or later in life, when they realized what their passion, purpose, or calling was. They knew right then what they should do with their lives and careers, but because they were operating from a passive point of view, they didn't seek that dream because of fear, hopelessness, or because they just didn't have the energy. Being passive takes a lot of energy.

Let's say you've always wanted to be a portrait painter, but are afraid that if you pursue your dream you'll become the proverbial starving artist—destitute and homeless. In reality what happens is that even if passive people live in a mansion, they become emotionally (if not financially) destitute because they didn't pursue their passion. This is what I call "soul compromise." This sort of deal making also sabotages relationships.

Of course, compromise allows us to live in society. It's a part of life. But the contention should be over what movie we see, what we have for dinner, where we go on vacation.

Instead, we're taught somewhere along the line that we should compromise our deepest desires, passions, dreams, and goals. We end up losing chunks of our essential selves until we hit a wall on which a mirror hangs—and we no longer recognize the stranger's face staring back at us.

If the soul is compromised decade after decade, there is increased passivity, resentment, anger, depression, and fear. No one really carries into future decades resentments about seeing more chick flicks than tough-guy films, but we do carry resentments and anger if we became machinists instead of lawyers, stayed in the family business versus being a stand-up comedian, lived in the city while all the while yearning to wear boots and a cowboy hat.

After reading *The Half-Lived Life,* you will easily be able to see where you committed this infidelity of the heart and in so doing adopted a glass-half-empty view of yourself in the world. This is the time to follow the thirteenth-century Persian poet Rumi's wise advice: "Let yourself be silently drawn by the strange pull of what you really love."

PART I

SOLVING THE PROBLEM
OF PASSIVITY

As defined in this book, *passivity* is the compulsion to pursue the opposite of what we say we want. This compulsion—if not identified and dealt with—sabotages success, leaves us unfulfilled at best, and at worst causes depression, hopelessness, and a feeling of being victimized.

"I don't care. Whatever you want is fine with me."

"It is not the job I want, but in this economy you really can't be choosy."

"He's not perfect but I'm thirty-five years old. Nobody's perfect. I'm sure we will grow into love."

"I'd love to write. I've always dreamed someday I'd write but I have kids and a job. Not everybody gets their dreams to come true. Maybe when I retire . . ."

> Passivity *is the compulsion to pursue the opposite of what we say we want.*

"I can't believe what is going on in Washington these days. They are all idiots and con men. But there's nothing an average Joe like me can do about it."

"Go ask your father. If he says yes, then it's okay."

"That's the way the cookie crumbles. It's just not in the cards. It's not God's will. I guess I'm just unlucky. Some people get all the breaks. It is what it is."

Does any of the above ring a bell? If so, there may be areas in your life where passivity rules your attitudes, behaviors, personality, and decisions. Perhaps you've settled for less than you felt you deserved, or you adapted to your present situation or relationship rather than changing it. Did you "cop out," give up, quit, and become hopeless and helpless, feeling like you were a victim of fate rather than a creator of your own destiny?

Unfortunately, many people have developed a connection to loss and feeling *less than;* they settle for unfulfilling relationships or careers that never quite let them achieve their creative potential. Surviving rather than thriving has become the state that many of us are not only used to, but compelled to pursue.

As one highly successful surgeon who was growing increasingly wary of settling said, "I always feel I am half the husband, half the father, half the friend, and half the doctor I know I can be even though I'm considered very successful in my field."

I said, "It sounds like you are living a half-lived life."

"Exactly! But I'm fifty years old. I don't want to say this at sixty or seventy. I want the second half of my life to be a much fuller, satisfying life, but I'm not sure how."

I'll tell you what I told him. You do this by coming out of denial, identifying the parts of your life where passivity prevails, working with the origins of your passivity, becoming aware of its signs and behaviors, and acquiring new but tried-and-tested tools, information, and insights that will serve as solutions so you can fully engage in life, work, relationships, creativity, parenting, grandparenting, and much more.

IDENTIFYING PASSIVITY

Almost no one reading this is purely passive. Most of us exhibit passive tendencies, which ultimately leave us feeling that our life or career glass is half empty.

We halfheartedly commit to projects, plans, and goals. Passive people are half in and half out of relationships. Those who suffer the effects of a half-lived life are more attached to *not* having what they think they want or desire, even though they protest loudly that this is not so.

Passive people are half in and half out of relationships.

A client of mine, James, is a very successful forty-year-old real estate agent who earns a high-six-figure income. During a session he said, "I work all the time on my marriage. I'm in therapy, I read books, and I regularly attend self-help workshops. No one can say I'm passive." When I asked about his marriage, he quickly replied, "I want more physical contact, more touching, and yes, more sex, but I hardly get any at all."

James wants his wife, Brenda, to be more affectionate, and yet he indulges in a whole host of behaviors that actually gets him the opposite of what he thinks and says he wants.

I asked him to give me an example of his efforts to get affection from his wife so I could see and show him the pattern of his passivity.

James said, "I go into the living room where Brenda is on the couch watching television for hours on end. I say something like, 'Can't you turn that thing off for a little while? There's nothing worth watching on TV. I don't know why you watch these silly shows.'"

I jokingly said, "How's that working for you?" Then I offered a suggestion. "Try sitting on the living room couch next to her, gently lifting her legs, and placing them on your lap while you massage her feet. Instead of shaming, criticizing, demeaning, and judging her, simply ask her what's on that you two can watch together."

He looked at me like I was speaking in a foreign tongue; in a way it *was* an unfamiliar language, because it was the language of compassion and assertiveness.

"No, I never even thought of it. It sounds so simple. Why didn't this ever occur to me before?" he said very seriously.

It was because of his passivity and his fears of rejection, abandonment, and intimacy.

By the way, he reported back the very next week. "Ten minutes after doing what you suggested, she looked at me and said 'Who are you?' Before I could answer she laughed and said, 'Never mind, I like this,' and we got up and got in bed and made love for the first time in a year."

This same man devoted an exorbitant amount of time to reading about relationships and marital counseling. He said he worked all the time on his marriage. But in reality, he thought his wife had the problem and not him.

Passivity, then, is an offense of omission—not doing or saying what you need to—rather than one of commission, and that is one reason why it has been overlooked by clinicians and writers.

Passivity compels people to wait in a state of suspended animation until something or someone outside themselves "rescues" them from their current circumstances; only then will they have the full life that has been eluding them. This knight in shining armor—whether a person, the world, society, or a supernatural being—is supposed to bring something they feel they have lost or had taken from them. That something could be hope, energy, love, trust, or faith. It could mean a perfect job, an unconditional lover, winning the lottery, or good parents. It is a psychological, physical, emotional, and spiritual condition that plagues even the most educated and self-directed people, and therefore the whole person must be addressed.

Passivity pushes people to replay the feelings and memories they've stored in their brains and bodies, possibly for decades. One of those feelings is of "Not Having What I Really Want or Need."

Sandra is a thirty-six-year-old life coach who has never been married. When asked what she wants out of life, she replies very quickly that it is to be a wife and a mother.

"It is what I was meant to do with my life," Sandra says.

Her whole romantic history says just the opposite. The last two men she was involved with were married with children. The man before that lived three thousand miles away; they had a long-distance relationship that lasted six years before he broke it off. Sandra keeps picking unavailable men. Her passivity drives her into the arms of those who are guaranteed not to give her what she says she longs for.

Passivity, then, is an offense of omission—not doing or saying what you need to.

When I point this out to her, she replies, "Are you sure it's not the men and their inability to commit?"

While I don't say an emphatic no, I tell her it's more likely that she is addicted to not having and getting negated by them.

Sandra knows how to be alone, be on her own, depressed and despairing. When I asked her about her childhood, she said, "It seems like I've been alone all my life. It's what I know."

Studies have shown that a child ages two through six hears eighty-five *no*'s for every *yes*.

"Mama, I need to go the bathroom."

"No you don't. You just went a few minutes ago."

No becomes a way of life. We even learn to say no to ourselves.

"Daddy, I'm hungry."

"You can't be hungry. We just ate."

"I'm not sleepy."

"Oh yes you are."

No becomes a way of life. We even learn to say no to ourselves. As my client said this morning during a consultation, "I know what I need to do but I don't do it. That is the story of my life."

Children who hear too many no's eventually withdraw and become apathetic, which later becomes a permanent character trait as a defense. These people do not make great team players. Their motto is: *Say nothing, do nothing, feel nothing.* Their behavior—or lack of it—eventually drives everybody a little crazy.

Passivity results because those who have their reality negated over and over begin to question their own minds, perceptions, and even bodily functions. Finally, they come to believe they simply don't have what it takes to immerse themselves in successful endeavors.

Self-doubt is a major sign of passivity. Douglas is a fifty-five-year-old house painter. He has a dozen men working for

Self-doubt is a major sign of passivity. him and makes a high-six-figure income. I have known him for ten years. Every time one of my books comes out, he calls to congratulate me. He goes on every time to say, "You know, I have always wanted to write a book. I have a lot of good stories from Vietnam."

I say, "You are a gifted storyteller. Write the book. I know you could do it. It would be a great book."

"You really think I could?"

"I know you can."

What Doug is really attached to is *not writing a book* and hearing me say over and over again that he could do it. He enjoys the validation I give his intelligence and his storytelling ability. In other words, he feels successful for a few moments—not fulfilled, but successful. Whereas if he wrote a book and couldn't get it published, or it wasn't a success, or if he tried to write and couldn't he would feel like the failure his father always told him he would be. One of Doug's dad's favorite things to say was that Doug "doesn't have shit for brains and will never amount to anything."

When I ask Doug, "Who are you the angriest at?" he never names his father. Rather—like nine of out ten people—he responds "myself" right off the bat. When I ask why, these are some of his and other people's answers:

- I'm not living up to my potential.

- I know what to do but I don't do it.

- I'm not as smart as I should be.

- I never went to college.

- I don't have any discipline.

- I'm not that good with money.

- I don't know what I want to do with my life.

- I make the same mistakes over and over.

- My father always said I'd never make it in the real world.

- I just don't have what it takes.

No wonder so many people settle for a half-lived life. If you are angry at yourself all the time, one way to punish yourself is to sabotage your ability to excel in the areas you're involved in—be that relationships, work, or artistic endeavors.

People who say they are angry at themselves are usually suffering from mild to extreme passivity. It is a negation of yourself, your dreams, your goals, and your success. Passivity is a personal, sometimes permanent and terminal absentee-ism from life. We're not *there* for ourselves because we are so *angry* at ourselves. At that point, passivity is self-aggression in its worst form. This self-aggression comes in many different disguises, ranging from self-hatred to low self-worth. Passive people are full of self-doubt and self-condemnation with tendencies to criticize everything they say, do, and think, especially when they perceive they have failed at something or not achieved their or someone else's goals or standards.

Passivity is a personal, sometimes permanent and terminal absenteeism from life.

In an early work of mine, *The Flying Boy Book II*, I state, "Adults can't be abandoned." When I say this at workshops or consultations, people look at me like I'm crazy. "What do you mean?" they'll respond, "I feel abandoned all the time," or "My ex-husband abandoned me," or "My parents [or children] have abandoned me."

Then I say, "I didn't say you couldn't feel abandoned, but the real abandonment you are usually expressing is the abandonment of yourself." Responses to this comment include excitement, groans, sighs, and tears. If we abandon ourselves continually, we will eventually feel that everyone and everything has abandoned us. And the passivity sinks even deeper into our souls and bones.

What Passivity Is Not

People who are deeply affected by untreated, undetected passivity are not procrastinators putting off until tomorrow what they know they need to do today. Men and women who display passivity are not ambivalent or lazy or apathetic. Indeed, it is just the opposite. Many passive people are type A personalities who are taking their kids to school and to soccer practice, working fifty or sixty hours a week, and climbing the ladder of success at breakneck speed. They have committed to unfulfilling jobs, adjusted to less-than-satisfying vocations, and settled for poor or mediocre relationships.

Passive people's creed is, "I'm bored with my job" or "I'm overwhelmed by all the housework and raising children." They think the world acts on them and moves them rather than being actors and movers themselves. Most passive people feel like they didn't really have a chance to pursue the life they really wanted; instead life forced them into their current roles—roles they would relinquish if they only knew how.

Passive people's creed is, "I'm bored with my job" or "I'm overwhelmed by all the housework and raising children."

Their passivity may wear the mask of laziness or procrastination, but here I'm talking about inaction on a deeper level. Laziness or procrastination is almost always a temporary problem that does not have relationship consequences and can be reversed with little effort. One of the main reasons real passivity is so difficult to identify is that one of the greatest tricks passive people play on themselves goes something like this:

"Look how hard I work. I work eighty hours a week and am the CEO of a large company. How can anyone label me as passive?" Or "Look how much I work on myself. I go to five 12-step meetings a week and see my therapist regularly. How can I be passive?" Or "Can't you see I'm suffering? Isn't that proof that I'm not attached to passivity?"

I asked the CEO who made those remarks, "If I called your teenage son and asked him to tell me who his father really is, what do you think he'd say?"

The hardworking man paused for several seconds and finally replied, "He'd say he didn't know. I don't spend that much time with him, probably not nearly as much as I should."

One of the main symptoms of passivity (we'll go into many more symptoms later) is being out of balance in our personal and professional lives.

MEN AND WOMEN UNDER THE INFLUENCE

Passive people constantly feel that something or someone is much stronger than them; they are merely pawns being moved around on this chessboard called life. Ironically, because they feel controlled and out of control, they tend to be labeled by friends, relatives, employees, and co-workers as "control freaks." Control freaks create the illusion they are in control by trying (not succeeding, mind you) to influence others' thoughts, actions, behaviors, and beliefs.

Jim is a thirty-five-year-old bank teller. He is single and lives in his mom and dad's garage apartment. His mom has a key. When Jim goes to work, his mom lets herself in and cleans, washes his clothes, and organizes his desk. Jim tells members of the workshop I am running that while he doesn't like that she does this, there is nothing he can really do because he doesn't want to hurt her feelings.

As Jim goes on to describe his mother, it becomes clear she is very passive in her relationship to Jim's father, who is a practicing alcoholic and work addict. "My father tells her pretty much what she can and cannot do, how much to spend, and even how much time she can be with friends." Needless to say Jim saw this behavior all his life and has taken after his mother.

Barry, fifty-eight, owns his own contracting business. He is a control freak at work. He never delegates unless absolutely necessary, and when he does he micromanages every move. He even admits he wishes he could let go of some control, given that he has had two heart attacks and his blood pressure is dangerously high. But when he gets home, it is altogether different. He acquiesces to his wife in every matter. She gives him a weekly allowance, monitors how much he drinks at night, tells him when he can play cards and for how long. They haven't had sex in two years; he doesn't even try anymore and instead waits for her to initiate. Before the children left home, she was in complete control of them as well.

Jason feels that cigarettes are stronger than he is. He will look you right in the eye and say, "I have no power over my cravings for nicotine." Beatrice says, "When it comes to food, I simply don't have a say." Thomas will be the first to tell you that alcohol is his "lord and master." These people are not just addicted to substances—they are addicted to the process of passivity. Overcoming passivity then becomes a key factor in fighting addictions and compulsions that end in pain, illness, and even death.

THE SYMPTOMS OF PASSIVITY

The men and women who are plagued by this problem "are troubled relatively little by the quagmire of passivity," says Edrita Fried in the preface to her book *Active/Passive: The Crucial Psychological Dimension.* She goes on to note that the passive person's main concerns focus on the symptoms rather than the cause. One of the main symptoms of passivity is depression. Recent statistics suggest that after age eighteen, roughly seven of every one hundred people suffer depression at some point in their lives. Most people diagnosed with major depression are diagnosed between their late twenties and mid-thirties. Of the some six million people affected by late-life depression, only 10 percent ever receive treatment. For every one man who develops depression, two women will—regardless of racial or ethnic background or economic status. By the year 2020 depression will be the second most common health problem in the world.

While there are more than eighteen million people in America suffering from depression, only 30 to 40 percent find that taking prescription drugs offers any relief. A good deal of depression is biochemical, but undetected passivity and repressed emotions may be causing depression in some of those not helped by medications. In all the lists and statistics I've found on depression, very little is really said about passivity being a factor.

If people are constantly feeling "acted upon" by "outside forces," they will become depressed.

According to *Webster's Sixth New Collegiate Dictionary,* passivity consists of being "not active, but acted upon; affected by outside force or agency [and] receiving or enduring without resistance or emotional reaction . . ."

A person being acted upon and affected by outside forces is one who allows circumstance and environment to dictate his or her state of mind. The question is: What are individuals really doing when they allow themselves to assume a passive stance?

Although the *Diagnostic and Statistical Manual of Mental Disorders,* fifth edition (commonly known as DSM-V), does not list passivity as a precursor to depression, if people are constantly feeling "acted upon" by "outside forces," they

Living as Someone Else Wants You to Live

Once there was a fine warren on the edge of a wood, overlooking the meadows of a farm. It was big, full of rabbits . . .

One day the farmer thought, "I could increase these rabbits: make them part of my farm—their meat, their skins. Why should I bother to keep rabbits in hutches? They'll do very well where they are.". . . He put out food for the rabbits, but not too near the warren. For his purpose they had to become accustomed to going about in the fields and the wood. And then he snared them—not too many; as many as he wanted and not as many as would frighten them all away or destroy the warren.

They grew big and strong and healthy, for he saw to it that they had all of the best, particularly in winter, and nothing to fear—except the running knot in the hedge gap and the wood path. So they lived as he wanted them to live and all the time there were a few who disappeared. The rabbits became strange in many ways, different from other rabbits. They knew well enough what was happening. But even to themselves they pretended all was well, for the food was good, they were protected, and they had nothing to fear but the one fear . . .

—WATERSHIP DOWN BY RICHARD ADAMS

will become depressed in only a matter of time. It is very interesting to note that the symptoms of passivity are almost identical to the signs of depression:

Symptoms of Depression and Passivity
Sadness that does not abate
Passive people are often sad in part because they do not actively grieve their missed opportunities, sabotaged relationships, stagnant careers, and much more. When depression is not biochemical, it is usually brought about by repressed and denied emotions that continually build.

Loss of interest in activities previously enjoyed
When people feel like they're bound to fail, or have been told from a young age that they can't succeed, they eventually withdraw from social, sports, and recreational activities and become more and more sedentary.

Unintentional weight gain or weight loss
The more people withdraw, the more their weight becomes a problem—and the more their weight becomes a problem, the more they withdraw. Passivity is a real catch-22. Comfort food—packed with calories and sugar—becomes increasingly important. Sugar is a contributing factor in depression and passivity.

Unhealthy sleep patterns

In some cases insomnia plagues the passive person. As lethargy sets in, sugar intake increases, and sleep cycles get out of whack. Other times passive people find that the only moment they are comfortable is when they are asleep, so they sleep as much as possible.

Energy loss

All of the above results in energy loss, a feeling of being tired and drained. Since energy is the key to active engagement with life, feelings of worthlessness increase, and passive people become irritable and hard to be around. They lose interest in sex and become constant complainers with unexplained ailments and excuses as to why they cannot be more engaged. They feel as if life has abandoned them.

Passive people become irritable and hard to be around.

Those around passive people eventually become frustrated with them, understanding their unrealized potential. They, too, become uninterested and eventually avoid their passive companions. As Fried points out, this includes the therapeutic community, who withdraw from treatment and refer their clients to other clinicians.

Depressed passive people may finally receive some help from non-therapy psychiatrists or personal physicians via antidepressants—which mostly mask the real problem, sometimes for decades.

If you're experiencing a half-lived life—not achieving, not engaging life, having little or no success in career, relationship, or creative endeavors—how could you *not* be depressed? If you're going to therapy for one hour per week and taking a serotonin reuptake inhibitor once a day but are living your waking life with a less-than-satisfying relationship, going to a job that holds little or no interest for you, wanting to be something you feel forever eludes you—how could you *not* be depressed by the passivity that plagues you?

Other Signs of Passivity
People pleasing

Many passive people turn into people pleasers who repress or hide their opinions, suggestions, criticisms, and comments for fear of alienating those around them even further. They very often speak disparagingly of themselves and superficially praise those they come in contact with, but with underlying resentment and rage. Passive people are constantly scanning the faces of those around them to see how to please them. These are also the ones who can never say the word *no*. They say *yes* to things they do not want to do—and once again we have a fertile field for resentment to grow.

Fixing

Passive people pleasers very often become co-dependent fixers. One major way to avoid dealing with our own passivity is to focus on everyone else's problems and pain. If fixers come up with solutions, cures, insights, then for a moment or two their self-esteem is raised. So they actually look for people who seem to need fixing or are broken in some way, and then they pour what little energy they have into them.

Passive people are usually full of rage, in large part because they feel other people and life itself have refused them in multiple ways.

Raging

Passive people are usually full of rage, in large part because they feel other people and life itself have refused them in multiple ways, ripped them off, dismissed them, ignored or neglected them. This rage is very often directed inward, though occasionally passive people can become very outwardly aggressive.

Aggressiveness

A small minority of passive people employ aggressive behavior and actions to try and prove to themselves and their world that they are not victims of life, love, and careers gone awry. At the far end of the spectrum, they can become violent, engaging in domestic violence and even homicide.

Narcissistic and grandiose behavior

Passive people can be narcissists who—although they feel like they don't have any value or self-worth—have grandiose fantasies about how they would do things if life or their bosses would only give them a chance. These fantasies are almost never grounded in reality.

Unresponsive body

In true passivity the body is unresponsive and sluggish. The knees are usually locked, lips are tightly closed, shoulders bowed in but very rigid. When passive people walk, they look like they are carrying or dragging a heavy load, and when they sit they tend to slump in their chairs.

Trite language

Passive people tend to use trite, clichéd language to describe or explain important things happening in their lives. Everything is "cool" or "fine," and a passive response to nearly everything is "whatever." Language is unoriginal and unimaginative because it takes a great deal of energy to be eloquent. Big events, major happenings, and even major losses are relegated to "It's all good" or "It is what it is."

Inert mind

Passive people can sink into inertness so completely that they cannot make connections between events and their causes. An example is a client who once said during a session that 9/11 was caused by Muslims and therefore he felt that all Muslims were secretly terrorists. The passive person's emotional and intellectual curiosity is practically nonexistent—hence the tendency to issue pat answers to very complex questions.

Fear of being overwhelmed

Those suffering from passivity are anxious and constantly worried that life, love, work, relationships, and friendships—you name it—will be too much for them and overwhelm them. This is because they know they have little energy to cope. They are afraid that they will be drained—and yet ironically they are the ones draining other people's energy. They are sometimes referred to as "psychic vampires."

Living vicariously

Passive people love movies, especially sad ones, which allow them to grieve for someone else's losses but not their own, and this does provide some temporary relief. While television is not a cause of passivity, it certainly is a symptom, as are simplistic novels, excessive computer games, and "virtual" anything—sex, war, crime, and so on.

The psychoanalyst Erich Fromm said, "A passive person . . . is an eternal suckling babe. What he consumes is ultimately of little consequence to him. Then he is gradually sated without having to do anything himself."

And yet I want to be clear that almost no one I have worked with can be labeled 100 percent passive. I'm sure such people exist, but what I've found in virtually every one of my clients and workshop participants, including very high-functioning, successful people, is myriad passive tendencies. Another psychoanalyst, Erik Erikson, said of such people that they "want to be users of life . . . And this urge to act on the environment and to effect movement and change is universal . . . One of the most basic needs of the human race is activeness. To tackle life, to make human contacts, to experience vivid emotions and to exercise will and skills are prime desires."

Almost no one I have worked with can be labeled 100 percent passive.

By understanding and identifying the signs of areas in our life that are plagued by passivity, we can become conscious "users of life"—our own prime movers who experience the full range of our emotions and are as actively engaged in life as we long to be.

In order not to end up like the protagonist in T. S. Eliot's poem *The Love Song of J. Alfred Prufrock,* and live with the constant question, "Do I dare disturb the Universe?" we must

> ## Signs of Passivity
> - *Poor or little memory.*
> - *Crucial events are minimized.*
> - *Few distinctions are made between peak and mundane experiences.*
> - *Self-doubt.*
> - *Self-criticism.*
> - *Self-hatred.*
> - *Addictions to substances and processes.*

look at the types of passivity, its origins, and the solutions (of which I am happy to report there are many).

THREE TYPES OF PASSIVITY IN CHILDREN

Passivity in childhood becomes assimilated in the adult's behavior and character. One or two of the above signs are usually more prominent than others. Both the obviously passive and the disguised passive type displayed one or more of the following passive styles when they were infants and early in their childhood.

Barrier Passivity

Barrier passivity is the result of children sending out signals that they are in discomfort that are not answered. They scream

Types of Adult Passivity

Obviously Passive People	Disguised Passive People
• *The shoulders are bowed toward the ground: They carry the weight of the world.*	• *The body is taut and tense.*
• *The chest is tight and constricted, and breathing is shallow.*	• *The knees are locked.*
	• *Speech is accelerated to a rapid-fire pace.*
• *Lack of self-confidence.*	• *Always hyperbusy.*
• *Minimal sense of mastery over danger.*	• *Overestimate talents and abilities.*
• *Feeling that destiny and fate control them.*	• *Feel superior to those around them.*
• *Nervous, angry, and full of anxiety.*	
• *Speak slowly and in clichés.*	
• *Crucial events are minimized.*	

and fret, but nothing happens. After many cries for help are not responded to, they finally find themselves behind a kind of emotional barricade of immobility and silence. These are the children who say, "Look, Mama, I'm dead." They play dead because at some level that's how they feel. Can you see the rage that results?

After many cries for help are not responded to, they finally find themselves behind a kind of emotional barricade of immobility and silence.

These children become adults who build walls and hide behind them, sometimes for decades. Husbands, wives, lovers, and even children try for years to penetrate these walls, to tear them down, go over or around or under them—to no avail. Sometimes during the romantic phase of a relationship, passive people will drop these walls temporarily to hook the one they are attracted to, only to restore the barriers once the object of affection is secured.

Plea Passivity

If a parent enjoys too much closeness with a child, the child may crave even more attention and intervention. Rather than nurturing and fostering separation, the child gets stuck in a high, unhealthy level of dependency, which leads to adults with extremely dependent personalities and a *Give me, Do it for me,* or *I'm entitled* stance in life. Their insatiable need for indulgence dramatically increases the likelihood that they will become addicts or alcoholics—one of the truest symptoms of passivity there is.

These kids are transformed into adults whose lives are one big plea for attention. No matter how much they get, it is never enough. They're what I call *Never enough* or *It's never good enough* people. No matter how much you do or give to them, it is just not enough or not good enough. They are forever buying bigger and better things, changing homes, jobs, or lovers, searching for the mother lode. They are constantly frustrated and angry because they never find what they are looking for, until finally they give up, having exhausted themselves and everyone around them.

Alibi Passivity

This is a very common form of passivity that children, especially teenagers, slip into. "My legs are too short to play basketball. If I had longer legs, I'd play and I'm sure I'd be great at it." "If I had received a better education, then I could have gotten into that Ivy League university." "No one in my family is good with math."

When they become adults, the rhetoric is similar: "I was raised on the wrong side of the tracks," "I don't have the time," "Maybe I'll follow my dream when the kids are out of school," "All the good ones are taken." Alibi passivity puts the blame on the environment or circumstances cloaked with a self-imposed lack of choice and possibilities. In other words,

Alibi passivity puts the blame on the environment or circumstances cloaked with a self-imposed lack of choice and possibilities.

it is everyone's fault but mine so don't blame me for having the affair, taking the bribe, reacting with violence—"they" made me do it. "Blame them not me." "I was just doing what I was told."

According to Edrita Fried, "Barrier passivity and plea passivity are both found in one person. The emerging character profile reveals alternations between insatiable demands for indulgence and stubborn refusals of friendly gestures that are offered . . . the passive person tries to extract unlimited indemnity for the mistakes made by parents, caretakers, and later substitutes."

CAUSES OF PASSIVITY

Like many psychological, emotional, and behavioral problems, passivity dates back to childhood. Passivity is a form regression takes when our unexpressed rage at being abandoned haunts us. It can only be exorcised when we've gotten the right amount of attention, empathy, time, connection, emotional release, and discharge, which I will say much more about later. Only then we can finally come "home" to ourselves. Once we actively commit to never abandoning ourselves again, then no adult can leave us feeling abandoned.

Many people have said to me, "But I was never abandoned as a child. I had good, loving parents, and yet I feel abandoned by many people in my life."

Take a few moments and on a sheet of paper answer the following questions as honestly as you can.

What walls are still in place in your life, and with whom?

_____

_____

What are you still pleading for and to whom?

_____

_____

What is it you would love to do—but you're still using old alibis for not doing so? _____

_____

What are you getting out of your passivity today?

_____

_____

What does your passivity cost you today?

_____

_____

Who do you need to make amends to given that your passivity hurt them? _____

_____

For most of the nineteenth and twentieth centuries (and to some degree today), childbearing was a medical or surgical procedure. Women were basically told the doctor knew what was best; the woman's connection to her baby's birth was taken totally out of the equation. Many women were anesthetized so deeply they often were unaware of what had occurred; the baby was often wrapped and swept away after only moments of bonding. That type of childbearing sometimes grew into disconnected child rearing, which created a subtle abandonment of the child—one that occurred quite a bit even in the most functional, loving families. We've all heard, "It takes a village to raise a child." Until modern times that's exactly who raised children—the entire community. Fifty percent of American families are now one-parent households. A two-person parenting household is not even close to a village, much less a one-parent home. Never before in the history of human beings have so few been required to give so much to so many. While these single-parent and even two-parent homes are often doing remarkable jobs of raising their children, the children are spending huge amounts of time alone.

Passivity is a form regression takes when our unexpressed rage at being abandoned haunts us.

Thanks to the industrial revolution, Dad is at work eight, ten, sometimes twelve hours a day. Stay-at-home mothers and workforce mothers both have a full-time job raising the kids and taking care of household duties that would be daunting for even a couple of full-time housekeepers.

Picture this disturbing but real-life scenario: There is food in the oven due to come out any minute, the oldest child just fell off her bike and comes in with a skinned, bleeding knee, the phone rings—and the two-year-old is screaming with a soiled diaper. Eager mouths and stomachs are waiting for a bottle or a breast. While it may take that hardworking, loving mother ten or fifteen minutes to get the food out, the phone answered, and the knee cleaned before that little one gets attention and contact, that amount of time is forever, eternal, and never-ending for the two-year-old. He may have no conscious memory of that time and many other times like it—yet he feels abandoned over and over, and he picks up the habit of abandoning himself after others have stopped. This rage and fear at being left is lying loose in his body and brain, and at some level a decision is made to make sure he never experiences those terrible, uncomfortable, and debilitating feelings again.

And yet passive people feel them continuously, this time by leaving themselves. In their passivity, they either let in no one who has the power to abandon them, or they push everyone away.

Another primary cause of passivity is the opposite of abandonment—smothering. Parents who are constantly hovering over their children—also known as "helicopter parents"—are unable to model secure boundaries. They produce children who are enmeshed with them and unable to separate, and who resort to passivity as a way to cope. These often well-intentioned parents overprotect, push, and prod their children to be winners, the best, a success, or super-achievers, but they are actually provoking many children into adult passivity.

Both the abandoned child and the smothered child are often full of anger, sadness, and hopelessness. These feelings go unacknowledged and unexpressed for decades under the plea that their parents "did the best they could," which is true for almost every person I've worked with: The parents *did* do the best they could with the information they had at the time.

Both the abandoned child and the smothered child are often full of anger, sadness, and hopelessness.

In 1946 Dr. Benjamin Spock wrote a revolutionary book on childcare that dubbed him "the Father of Permissiveness" for saying crazy things like "Children should be respected," and "Take it easy, trust your own instincts." Despite Dr. Spock's groundbreaking work on child rearing, many baby boomers were brought up by the previous generation's conventional wisdom, which said that you shouldn't pick up or coddle a crying infant, toilet training should start as soon as possible, and punishment is the only way to teach a child the difference between right and wrong. Or, as believed by my parents' parents and articulated in a turn-of-the-twentieth-century child-rearing manual, "If your child displays exuberance be sure to curb that behavior or risk that child becoming a sociopath."

Passive people—whether they were originally abandoned or smothered—very often enter a perpetual state of waiting. They wait for the "love object" (to use a neo-Freudian term) to return but never mourn or get angry about the original or primal loss. This love object is the parent they are less bonded to—where there is little bonding there is almost always bondage, and the passive captive waits to be set free. In my experience, both abandoned and smothered children grow up to be enraged adults who become self-sabotaging, picking or pushing away people that remind them of childhood parenting styles. Or they go to the opposite extreme and isolate and never fully engage in relationships at all, which makes everyone involved scared and confused at best.

Daniel is a client who picks the same love interest over and over again. "It's like I can't break out of picking women who leave me for another man, another city, or another job. It's like I'm picking women who are similar to my dad, who left me and Mom when I was twelve. He had a whole different family whom he paid a great deal of attention to and only sent us the occasional birthday or Christmas card with a check stuck in."

Linda said, "My mother was always on top of me. It's like I couldn't take a breath without her. I don't think I have any childhood memories that don't also include my mother being right there. I swore I'd never be that mother to any of my three children. We were in family therapy a couple of years ago and the two oldest boys—one then twelve and the other fifteen—said, 'Mom you were never there for us. Where were you?' I said I just wanted to give you boys the space I never had to grow and be your own person."

PASSIVITY IN MEN

Very little has been written about passivity in men—especially the particular form that Freud and others have called "the Masculine Protest." Yet we have recently made some headway—or I should say *heart way*—in understanding it.

For centuries men have been told (and many have been convinced) that passive equals feminine. Because our modern culture has oppressed women and seen them as the "fairer" or "weaker sex" (a view that has changed for most people born after the late 1960s), femininity was something to be feared; a negative characteristic to be avoided at all costs. In their attempt never to be seen as feminine, many men turn their backs on anything that smacks of it—especially emotions. This explains in part why many men's emotional intelligence is so stunted. Rather than being seen as passive or feminine, many men become hypermacho, hyperactive, aggressive, and money-driven.

In the play *Twelve Angry Men* (televised in 1957), juror number ten exemplifies this view when he says with absolute disdain, "What do you want us to do, sit here all night and discuss our feelings?" If men have little or no access to their emotions, and confident women are still called bitches or worse if they show too much assertiveness or anger, then rage will be the result and passivity will be the wall we hide behind.

Ken said to me during a phone consultation, "I stay busy all the time. Even when I get ready to go jogging to relax and unwind, I change clothes in the car at stop signs and red lights. I'm running all the time. Yesterday I woke up crying when I remembered a dream about my ex-girlfriend. I know this sounds silly, but I thought, *What if I'm gay?* That would explain why I'm forty-six and never married. If I spent any time examining the answer to this question all I could think of was all the women I could have dated, which would prove I'm not—not feminine like my dad always said I was, gay, or passive. So I jumped out of bed and I didn't stop working at my office until twelve that night."

Rather than being seen as passive or feminine, many men become hypermacho, hyperactive, aggressive, and money-driven.

Countless anonymous sexual encounters can be a smoke-screen for ignoring passivity, feelings of being inferior, or fear of appearing too feminine. These are the kinds of feelings men have been projecting onto women for a long time, resulting in rage on the part of both sexes.

The rejection of all things associated with "the feminine" is one of men's greatest regressions. The anger and disappointment it creates in women is to be expected and no longer needs to be denied to foster more adult behavior. Men, too, must face the unhealthy education and indoctrination they received as boys regarding the feminine. For compassion to replace fear of castration or being labeled gay, sissy, pansy, and other juvenile tags, regard, respect, and appreciation of the feminine—wherever it is found—must be modeled by both adult men and women for our children's sake, if not our own.

The passive man, or the man who fears being seen as passive because it has come to be associated with feminine traits, must go back into his history as soon as possible. There he can experience the unexpressed feelings he had when someone in some way questioned his masculinity.

The rejection of all things associated with "the feminine" is one of men's greatest regressions.

I recently spoke with Robert Bly, one of America's best poets and storytellers, and the unofficial father of the men's movement, at a men's gathering. There one of the participants, Brad, told of being six years old. "One night I went into the living room where my dad was watching a ball game and drinking with some guys who worked for him. I leaned over and tried to kiss him good night. He turned to me with whiskey on his breath, then looked at his drinking buddies and said, 'Now, aren't you the little girl? You don't ever kiss a man, I don't care who it is.' If that didn't take something out of me, the next statements tore a hole in my soul. 'Would you fellas look at my little girl here? Isn't she sweet? What do you think about a boy still wanting to kiss his father, a big boy like him? From now on you shake hands and never, ever let me see you kiss a man again or I'll break you into little pieces. Now get to bed, you little sissy.' There was something gone in me after that. I never trusted him again, or other men, and I have always questioned my sexuality—not to mention my masculinity."

Brad's emotional release and discharge of his rage and grief was so powerful that afternoon that it sent shivers down the spines of many of the men at the conference, who had experienced many different kinds of rejection of the gentler parts of themselves.

Due to poor parenting and less-than-satisfying experiences with fathers, many men have floundered and become powerless in the force fields of their overprotective or needy mothers. This, too, leaves them feeling an over-attachment to things feminine and therefore a fear of passivity.

I was having lunch the other day in a small cafe. A waiter, whom I judged to be in his early thirties, was talking to three women. It was after the lunch crowd had left, so he could relax and enjoy the everybody-knows-everybody-and-nobody's-in-a-rush way of a small town. I listened a bit to their conversation. At one point my ears really perked up. The young man said he had recently played a role in a local production of a Neil Simon play. "I had to cuss several times in the play," he said. "When my mother was in the audience, I was terrified. She'd never heard me talk like that."

I stopped listening for a moment to place my order. When I tuned in again, I heard him say: "I'm a big Monty Python fan. They did a great takeoff on Christianity in *The Life of Brian*, and they were wonderfully sacrilegious in *Holy Grail*. My mother wouldn't allow me to see either one when they first came out. To this day I don't dare tell her they're some of my favorites—I can't tell her I've even seen these movies."

As I sipped my coffee, I began to wonder. Was this young man showing respect for his mother? Did the women listening to him admire and respect him for being such a good son, a passive "good little boy"?

I hear adult sons say all the time that they'd like to tell their mothers all kinds of things. When asked why they don't, they reply: "It wouldn't do any good." "It would upset her too much." "It would just kill her." The son who was raised solely or mostly by the mother sinks deep into passivity and comes to believe that the feminine power she has over him is immense. He is always editing, censoring, and hiding parts of himself out of fear of what he thinks she'll think.

A more scholarly example of Mother's perpetual influence comes to us from the ancient stories of the real Holy Grail.

In his important book *He,* Robert Johnson does a masterful job of illuminating and interpreting this myth. The Grail, as Johnson says, is the "great cornucopia of life." It pours out its abundance and blessings on humankind. This is, in his opinion, the positive feminine that should scare no man. The one who finds it is Parsifal, whose name means "innocent fool." Parsifal is born to a woman named Heart's Sorrow.

His father is absent, and he is raised by his mother. As Johnson points out, "The redeeming hero in mythology often has no father and is raised in humble and lonely circumstances."

Heart's Sorrow keeps the boy with her, flooding him with her feminine energy, always fearful that someday he'll want to be a knight like his father and brothers and she'll be left alone. Sure enough, one day Parsifal sees five knights in full armor and is so impressed that he decides to join them. His mother bursts into tears, realizing she has failed to keep her son from discovering the ways of men.

How many of us men today have seen some kind of knights ourselves and felt a similar longing? These "knights" might have appeared in the form of a football hero, a poet, a doctor, a soldier in a war movie, or a telephone lineman. When we saw them we thought, *I would dearly love to go and become a "rider"—a writer, a star, a soldier—myself. But I would have to break free of the passivity and the mother that binds me and leave her behind, and she depends on me. So I'll passively take a job at the local factory instead. I'll move into a house just down the road or to her basement. I'll come up every evening to check on her and we'll have dinner together every Sunday until we die.* Should this man ever take a wife, he will almost always put his mother's wishes before hers, and she will forever be resentful.

Unable to hold Parsifal any longer, Heart's Sorrow lets him go. But before he leaves she gives him a garment she has woven for him. The garment is very fine and lightweight, in contrast with the heavy metal of the armor he will soon wear over it. I believe the homespun garment symbolizes the mother's smothering overprotection, and ultimately his fear of anything that smacks of the feminine. But it is also a literal coating of passivity insulating a man from the world around him. As long as we wear these things, we men remain passive, disconnected, and distant from those we wish to be close to.

Dear John:
I see my passivity in my life is around my behavior that involves sex, money, and anger. I say I want a truly intimate sexual relationship with the woman I have lived with for four years. And yet I constantly avoid facing and dealing with the conflicts that if resolved would

lead to deeper trust and intimacy. I will do anything to keep from facing any situations that involve conflict and confrontation. I know anger scares me but I think what scares me even more is being disapproved of. This is a constant theme and behavior in my life.

Thanks for the workshop. I think I at least have a good grasp of passivity and how it plays out in my life.

Best wishes,

William B.

John:

Thanks so much for the workshop on passivity. It really opened my eyes. Asking us to write about and examine these very uncomfortable behaviors gives me a feeling like I am still a little boy looking for sympathy, to be rescued and soothed from the mother or father I never had. It also makes me feel angry and misunderstood and I would feel hopeless if you hadn't provided a number of solutions and approaches to passivity.

All the careful list making I do every day and then the promises I make to myself and others to complete them will not solve my passivity problem and help me get what I say I want.

The level of denial I have in this area of my life is huge. I too often try and convince myself I am doing what I need to be doing to get what I want and am continually getting the opposite.

Thank God there is light at the end of this dark tunnel.

Take care and keep up the workshops,

Benny C.

PASSIVITY IN WOMEN

Passivity is obvious in many women, especially those born in the early and late twentieth century. The mothers of many baby boomers were indoctrinated into their passive roles. They were supposed to be the women who suffer quietly in the kitchen or the bedroom and never try to gain access to the boardroom because that would be too aggressive and unladylike. Thanks to the women's movement in the 1960s and '70s, women can now suffer in the boardroom or on the battlefield and be as aggressive, pseudo-aggressive, and passive-aggressive as many men were trained and encouraged to be. However, with all the bad and good things that came with all of this clear movement towards conscious equality, they still are encouraged to not get too angry or too assertive. But progress has been made.

Although passivity in the bedroom has been studied and written about with regard to women, passivity in general as it impacts women's lives has not. While the battle between nature and nurture is still being waged, it is accepted by many that the early relationship between mother and daughter forms the core of a woman's personality. While most mothers want nothing but the best for their daughters and for them to be accorded "first class" citizens' rights, there are many mothers who

The early relationship between mother and daughter forms the core of a woman's personality.

were raised to believe that women were not the equal of men. With time this, too, shall pass away into distant memory, much like the Freudian diagnosis of "hysteria."

But the truth is, there are unmotherly mothers out there. These mothers go a long way toward producing anxiety, sadness, guilt, and depression in their daughters. These daughters in turn find their way into passivity as a way to cope.

"To be a mother's daughter is a dangerous fate when the mother herself had inadequate maternal care," says Edrita Fried. Many times these daughters fall into one of four categories:

1. The daughter who becomes mother to her mother

This relationship breeds a certain kind of benign passivity by setting the woman up to be caretaker par excellence. The girl nurtures, protects, second-guesses her mother's needs, wants, and wishes, and is there to fulfill them as best as she can.

2. The daughter as mother's best friend

The mother is so immature that she and her daughter act, behave, think, and even dress alike. The mother confides in her daughter regarding age-inappropriate and extremely personal issues. This mother is often attracted to her daughter's young boyfriends, flirting and embarrassing her daughter.

3. The hyper daughter

This woman covers up her depression, apathy, sadness, and anger with hyperactivity. She thinks at a fever pitch, speaking rapidly and tending to exaggerate as she struggles to be seen as more powerful than she really is. Her manners and appearance change as often as her boyfriends, bosses, or friends. She is the eternal girl and never quite grows up.

4. The evil stepmother

This daughter suffered from poor mothering, and as a way to hide her inner weakness she shifts her suffering onto her victims. She takes on the role of victor, boss, or witch and steps on anyone she deems weak and unable to defend themselves. She humiliates her employees and deals out blows to her victims. She is the wicked stepmother in fairy tales, or the witch who throws children into a pot to boil and be hurt the way she was hurt.

Most all of these passive types "suffer" for love, are starved for attention, and have a masochistic strain in their character. They often are too tired for real relationships, fail at most of what they try, and eventually suffer from deep depression. They can become angry and even suicidal, but most of all they constantly feel misunderstood.

Perhaps none of these labels applies to you or your wives, lovers, mothers, or daughters. That is because there are huge numbers of women who are neither suffering nor weak. Their mothers set examples that enriched their daughters' lives. These mothers were full of energy and enthusiasm, and they loved to mother their daughters. These daughters become resilient and functional lovers, wives, mothers, and friends. They are the daughters of accepting mothers.

There are huge numbers of women who are neither suffering nor weak.

These women may demonstrate what I call passive tendencies rather than passive personalities. In other words, they are only passive in one or two areas of their lives, areas often harder to identify because their lives work so well in many ways. By middle age, though, their lives work a little (or a lot) less well, and the passivity rises to the surface and needs to be dealt with. The solutions to passivity that I will present in the second section of this book will be just as applicable to these women as they are to those with more severe passive personalities.

From Psychology to a Fairy Tale . . .

Once upon a time a king decided it was time to find his ugly snake son a bride and get him married so his golden-haired son could get married and inherit the kingdom. So he looked all around his kingdom for a suitable bride. He put an ad in the classifieds saying, "Single, slithery snake seeking lifelong partner. Poor table manners and too many other bad habits to mention." You'd be surprised how many takers there were. Passive women came out in droves. Some women loved snakes, it seemed, especially the tall, dark, handsome, and wounded ones, with lots of intensity and potential.

A beautiful bride was selected, and the pair got married. On the wedding night, though, the snake ate his bride. Why? Because she was so poorly mothered that she didn't know what to do. She passively gave in to the snake's demands. The king ran another ad, an unbelievable number responded, there was a wedding, and again the snake ate his bride on the wedding night. And so it went with the third, fourth, and fifth brides. As people began hearing about the snake's taste in women, new brides were getting a little harder to find.

There lived in the land a woodcutter's daughter who was extremely in touch with her own emotions and anything but passive. She decided to go for it. Unlike her predecessors, she actively sought out the wise old woman and asked her for advice. This was gladly given, along with the admonition to follow instructions to the letter or the young woman could also become snake food. The wise old woman's advice: to take her time and not rush into anything; to make seven beautiful wedding blouses and wear them on her wedding night; and to take a bucket of sweet milk and a steel brush with her to the bedroom. The young woman took about a year making her blouses. Waiting makes impatient snakes hungry. When the wedding night came, the snake closed the door, ready to have some wife food, but first he wanted a little pre-dinner show. He said, "Take off your blouse."

"I'll take off my blouse if you will take off one of your skins," she replied.

"Do what? You got to be kidding. That would hurt like hell. Besides, no one has ever asked me to do that before." But due to his hidden desire for real love, he began taking off his skin—and you should have heard the shrieks, cries, and yelling. You know it hurts to shed a skin. It also hurts to learn how to love.

When he was done, the woodcutter's daughter took off her blouse, only to reveal another one under it. The snake was perplexed and a little frustrated.

"Take off the blouse," he growled.

"I'll take off my blouse if you will take off your skin."

"I can't believe you're asking me to do all this stuff. None of the women I've eaten, I mean loved, ever asked me to do this. What do you want from me? Emotional honesty, availability? What next? I suppose you want me to open up and tell you what I really feel?"

So once again there was moaning and groaning as the snake shed another layer of skin. The woman removed her second blouse, only to reveal another one. Well, the snake was getting pretty irritated. This woman was not going to be as easy as the other brides; she knew how to take care of herself and ask for what she wanted, and she wouldn't settle for anything less than what she deserved. This went on until finally there was nothing left of the snake except a little puddle of his former self lying on the floor.

The bride took her bucket of sweet milk out from under the bed, dipped her steel brush into it, and scrubbed what remained of the snake for an hour or so. She had prepared herself to love him well, and in so doing prepared herself to be well loved. The next morning the wedding chamber doors opened and out stepped a beautiful, stunning prince with his smart, respected bride. They got the family together and had a great feast and lived happily ever after.

The snake didn't know the previous women he married and then ate. Carl Jung refers to these women as the "False Brides." The "True Bride," the maiden with the seven blouses, took her time, took care of herself, set boundaries, and knew her limits. She demanded that the snake/man *mourn his losses in order to truly know himself and her. The snake thought that he was simply a giant snake, but there was so much more to him. His bride was prudent and patient enough with him that he found out just who his true self really was.*

Can you identify the passivity in the story? Have you or has someone you know been one of the brides who was devoured in a relationship? Have you or has someone you know gone way too fast because passive people also tend to be impatient people? How is the snake passive? How is the woodcutter's daughter not displaying passivity?

John Lee:

One of the main areas where my passivity really shows up the most is in trying to meet everyone else's needs rather than focusing on what I need to do to get what I want. I will have a list of things to do that will create money for me and my husband and children but then I will let other projects and people come before them. Lord only knows what I get out of this behavior because I sure don't. Is what you're saying that I am afraid to do something else for fear that I might not fail and really succeed in my life?

This is a real problem for me but it is not only me who suffers. I don't know why someone hasn't pointed out this passivity problem to me before. I've done every kind of therapy you can name. At least now I can see clearly how to come out of this.

With gratitude,

Beth Ann G.

Dear John:

You asked us at the workshop what we get out of our passivity. My compulsive behavior around my passivity gets me lots of attention but definitely not the kind I say I want. My passivity around my sex life is a very troubling area for me. I continually do not set aside time and give hardly any energy to make love to my husband. I say I want an intimate and sweet sexual relationship with him and then I neglect him sexually. I blame it on me being too busy, or him being too tired or my low libido. I want him to make time for me and initiate intimacy and sex. This is another example of doing the opposite of what I say I want.

Thank you for the tools you gave us in the workshop. Now all I have to do is use them.

Sincerely,

Rhonda J.

PART 2

THE SOLUTIONS

*Wholly unprepared, we embark upon the second half of life
... worse still we take this step with the false assumption
that our truths and ideals will serve as before. But we
cannot live the afternoon of life according to the program
of life's morning—for what was great in the morning will
be little at evening and what in the morning was true will
at evening have become a lie.*

—CARL JUNG

REMEMBERING WHO YOU WANTED TO BE

Remember in your teens or twenties picturing how your life
was going to be? It didn't quite turn out that way, did it?
Many have lived a much smaller life than they planned. If you
take away the children and the paycheck, the smallness too
often becomes apparent. And yet even now you know in your
heart of hearts there is still so much life in you wanting to
burst forth.

It is time to answer the question, *Why did I get so much
life only to use such a small portion of it?* How do we release

all these feelings that have been stored up, swallowed, and repressed for so long? How do we regain hopes that have been heaped and collected in the backs of our minds, and turn them into realities? Many people get lost in all this unused life.

It is time to remember who you really want to be. You have just the right amount of time left to be it.

So dry your tears and pat yourself on the back for recognizing the truth and coming out of half-dead denial. It is time to pull out those dreams that have been boxed up inside your sleepy brain and dust them off. You got too used to being "the mother," "the wife," "the father," "the husband," "the boss," or "just another working stiff."

It is time to remember who you really want to be. You have just the right amount of time left to be it.

INFIDELITY OF THE HEART

In order to begin, we first have to know all the ways we committed what the poet David Whyte called "infidelity of the heart"—how we cheated ourselves out of a full-glass life. The journey starts in what for some will be the unlikeliest of places: by digging in the fields of poetry, mysticism, and psychology. Most of us have put off looking in these places because some English teacher in high school or college kept pushing the DHM (Deep Hidden Meaning) approach to poetry, and when we didn't get it we gave up. Or perhaps you were taught to fear mysticism by a minister, priest, or rabbi, who preached only the gospel according to them. Maybe you came to believe psychology was as much a mystery as poetry and the mystic's way of life. I'm going to keep it simple, because I grew up with all these fears and misunderstandings myself and put off any serious study of these disciplines until well into my thirties.

Here is an excerpt from a lovely poem titled "A Story That Could Be True," by William Stafford.

> *The people go by—*
> *You wonder at their calm.*
> *They miss the whisper that runs*
> *Any day in your mind,*
> *"Who are you really, wanderer?"—*
> *And the answer you have to give*
> *No matter how dark and cold*
> *The world around you is:*
> *"Maybe I'm a king."*

Let's do an exercise. Close your eyes and take a couple of deep breaths. I want you to pretend you are standing at a gate at the airport of a strange city. A stranger walks up to you and says, "Who are you, wanderer?"

How do you answer?

Growing up in the South, Darren was taught that he should always remain humble and never behave in a way that could be considered proud, boastful, or arrogant. Darren, who is now in his early sixties, said during a session that as a deacon in the First Baptist Church in his small Tennessee hometown

The Story of the Fearful Frog

There was a frog who had never left his pond. One day he happened to meet an ocean frog who was traveling around. The ocean frog said to the pond frog, "Have you ever seen the ocean?" The pond frog didn't know what he was talking about. The ocean frog tried to describe it but could not. The pond frog thought leaving the pond he knew so well was a big risk; a huge gamble. "Look at what I'll be giving up if I go off in search of the ocean—security, comfort, recognition. I'm a pretty big frog in this little pond, but tell me again what the ocean is like and I'll think about it." The ocean frog shook his head. "I can't really explain what it is like where I live, but someday I'll take you there."

—Anonymous

he was taught never to praise himself but only to praise his "Lord and Savior." "I could never think I was a king," he said after reading the entire above poem. "Wouldn't that be—what do you call it—narcissistic?"

I replied that it would be what my friend and my colleague, psychoanalyst Dr. Robert Moore, calls positive grandiosity. Everyone has heard and been forewarned about negative grandiosity, the tendency to think more highly of oneself, one's character, personality, skills, or talents, but few have ever thought about, much less identified themselves as, being positively grandiose. What this means, if I understand Robert, is that we all have some gold in us that we ought to let shine. We should be proud of it and never let anybody put us down or criticize us for doing so. Isn't this sort of like the parable in the Bible that tells us we shouldn't hide our light under a bushel?

By letting passivity rule our lives, we have cheated on our own hearts—but there is no reason to feel guilty. Feeling guilty is what passive people do to keep their passivity going. We are way past this now. As the Persian poet Rumi says, "Why should we grieve that we've been sleeping? It doesn't matter how long we've been unconscious. We're groggy, but let the guilt go. Feel the motions of tenderness around you, the buoyancy."

In another poem, Rumi says,

All day I think about it,
Then at night I say it.
Where did I come from,
And what am I supposed to be doing.

Over the last couple of years of presenting the Half-Lived Life workshop to hundreds of people, one thing became obvious—most people knew exactly what they wanted to do and be somewhere between the ages of nineteen and twenty-five. This was before the family came, the credit card bills came, the forty- to sixty-hour workweeks came.

Feeling guilty is what passive people do to keep their passivity going.

You remember you wanted to go to Broadway or Hollywood to become an actor and win lots of recognitions, rewards, and money. You are now fifty-five, living in a suburb, and holding down a job to support your family. But if you listen to your soul and try out for community theater or go to your local community college and take acting courses, your heart will thank you for it. Or perhaps you wanted to be a veterinarian; you are now sixty-two. Well, fulfill that dream by getting certified as a vet's assistant. You wanted to be a highflying field correspondent for a national newspaper? Start your own blog and report the news that interests you at forty-seven. Trust the poet David Whyte's words, "When your vision is gone no part of the world can find you. Give up all the worlds in which you live except the one you own."

SILENCING THE DETRACTORS AND CEASING THE DISTRACTIONS

The poet T. S. Eliot says in his poem "Ash Wednesday," "Teach us to care and not to care and to be still . . ." Very often it is the noisy exterior or interior detractors and the ever-present distractions that take us away from our calling, our purpose, our mission, our very selves. The detractors can be the people who love us the most, as you will see below.

What are your distractions? Is it work, money, relationships, success, fame, reputation? The Persian poet Rumi says, "In every corner of the heart there is an idol waiting to be worshipped."

Perhaps your distractions are sickness, tiredness, or feeling burned out. David Steindl-Rast, a Catholic priest who works in India, says, "The antidote to exhaustion is not always rest." Sometimes you have to persevere and push to come out of passivity and grab hold of life. And yes, I know you may be tired of pushing.

After twenty-five years of counseling and coaching, I've realized there are eight primary reasons people give for not pursuing their dreams, no matter what age they are:

- Money
- Children
- Work
- Parents
- Friends
- Colleagues
- Religion
- Self-talk

Money

First let's deal with money. Most people with large amounts of money commit infidelity of the heart. In other words, they don't tend to do what they love or are passionate about any more than the person making thirty thousand a year or less.

Jerry is a pilot for one of the leading package delivery companies. He has had two heart attacks, and has been fined for drinking on the job and being unfit to fly; if he has one more episode, he will be terminated. His marriage is in a shambles. But because he started with the firm and got in on the ground floor, he makes a little over two hundred thousand dollars a year. He has two years until retirement at age sixty-three. During our consultation I asked if he enjoyed working and flying for the company.

"No. I hate every minute of it. I get to my destination, check into a hotel, drink and watch television, and stop drinking just in time to fly."

"What would you rather be doing?" I asked.

He didn't even stop and think before replying, "I've always wanted to own my own flight school and teach people how to fly. I love to fly—I just don't like flying for this job. Teaching people how to fly—boy, that would be the life."

"So why don't you do it?"

"Well, I got two more years to retire at full pension. If I wait, I get $220,000 a year."

"What if you retired today?" I said.

"I'd only get $180,000 a year and that wouldn't be enough to get the condo at the golf course my wife and I have been looking at and wanting for some time. But if I wait two years then we can get it."

This is not the first client who showed this kind of spiritual and emotional arrogance. He had legal troubles, an alcohol problem, and his wife was on the brink of filing for divorce. Why did he assume he had two years to waste?

Then there was Ronnie, a guy I grew up with who was more like a brother than a friend. Ronnie was an extreme extrovert, good looking, and captain of the football team. He and another friend went into business after he got back from Vietnam and made a killing in the construction business. At age fifty he had two beautiful boys, a gorgeous wife, and a mansion, and he sold his business for a cool profit of fifty million dollars.

I asked him one day at his five-star hunting retreat what he wanted to do with all that money. In between sips of Grey Goose vodka, he answered, "I don't know, John. I really don't know. But I have had this idea for a screenplay that has been in my head for years, and I want to hire you to write it for me." Hear the passivity ever so clearly?

I replied, "Why don't you write it yourself? You have all the time in the world and you have plenty of money."

"I can't write. You're the writer."

I pointed out that he could take a screenwriter's course with any master in this country or go back to college and get a degree in filmmaking.

"No. You don't understand, John. Fifty million isn't that much these days. I'm going to go back to work and open another company, and when I get a hundred million then I'll have enough for my kids. Then I'll figure out what I want to do."

I told him: "You already know what you want to do. You just need to do it."

Ronnie never wrote the screenplay, never went back to work. He died six months later from a heart attack.

When I ask my clients what they want to do, many know the answer. But as soon as it comes out of their mouths, so does something about money. When I ask, "If I wrote you a check right now for millions, would you do what you really believe you were meant to do?" most say yes. The fear of not having enough money is one of the major precipitators of infidelity of the heart for many good-intentioned men and women.

More people actually end up doing what they love not when they get more money, but just the opposite—after they are laid off, fired, divorced, or suffer some other catastrophic event.

If you are fifty or older and have been downsized, let go, terminated, and tortured while looking for new employment, you might want to consider Ernie Bjorkman. The longtime news anchor was comfortable with his quarter-million-dollar-a-year salary—that is, until he was told the TV station he worked for didn't need his services or his smile any longer. But like many of you reading this right now, Bjorkman had a secret passion—animals.

The fear of not having enough money is one of the major precipitators of infidelity of the heart.

When he was younger, he had a yearning to be a veterinarian. Bjorkman enrolled in a program at the Community College of Denver at the tender young age of fifty-eight and became a veterinary technician with a starting salary of a whopping thirty thousand. He says he loves working with and helping sick animals: "I think, I think . . . ask me a year from now . . . I'll be just as happy if not happier."

Children

The second most common excuse people give for not following their passions is their children. Cynthia is a robust, energetic woman who always wanted to be a recording artist. She has the talent, to be sure, but her husband is anything but supportive of her dreams to be a singer-songwriter. When I asked what kept her from going to Nashville and spinning the wheel of fortune or failure, she was quick to answer: "If it wasn't for the children I'd do it, but I have to think of them." Cynthia's daughters are thirteen and sixteen and won't be headed to college for a few years. "When they go to college, then I'll give it a try despite what my husband thinks or wants."

I said to Cynthia, "Do you know what you're modeling for your teenage daughters?"

"That I'm a good mother, I hope," she replied.

"You are also teaching them to defer their dreams for their husbands or boyfriends. If your children were three or five or even ten to twelve, maybe, but they are quickly becoming young adults. Remember, children don't take after strangers."

Work

Work is the next justification many use for not following their dreams. Roger is a carpenter who wants to be a painter. He got his BFA from a liberal arts college in Connecticut and tried showing his work at arts-and-crafts fairs on the eastern seaboard but couldn't make a "decent living." He got a job as a carpenter's helper when he was twenty-one and now makes, according to him, "a damn decent living." He is fifty years old. I asked him during a session how things were going and he said, "Well, I have high blood pressure, my cholesterol is out of sight, I'm about thirty pounds overweight, and I haven't had sex with my wife in six months. But we have a nice house, two new cars, and a log cabin in the mountains, and I'm not a day behind in my bills. So I guess all in all I'm doing all right."

"When is the last time you painted anything and sold it?" I asked.

"Ten years ago. I'd give anything if I could do it full-time, but who would pay the bills? My wife doesn't work, and I have a kid in college."

Sunil's father thinks he knows what is best for his son. "My father and mother would disown me if I just dropped what I'm doing and pursued what my dad calls a 'harebrained idea' and went back to school so I could go to seminary. I'm fifty-eight for God's sake. I have worked for my father at his marina in south Alabama since I was twelve. He keeps telling me that I will run it someday but he's eighty-two and shows no sign of slowing down. Every time I bring up the idea of going back to school, he says, 'Look, just give a healthy donation to the church, you're already on the board, you're serving the Lord, you're not a kid anymore.' The sad thing is, his company has made so much money that he and I both could quit work right now and live comfortably. He's even had a number of offers to buy him out. But he keeps hanging on, and I guess I do, too."

Friends and Co-dependency

Friends—or at least so-called friends and colleagues—are another reason why many people do not attempt to "follow their bliss." This is due to a fear that is almost never identified or talked about anywhere—the fear of Who Do You Think You Are. This is related to a disease that became popularized in the 1980s by people like Melody Beattie, best-selling author of *Codependent No More,* and Pia Mellody, a master therapist and author—co-dependency. Unfortunately, while

---

The World's Oldest Student

So you think you are too old, too over the hill, or just too tired to go back to school? Consider Nola Ochs, who graduated with a degree in history a few years ago. She was ninety-five years old and she's not stopping. Mrs. Ochs went back to Fort Hays State University in Hays, Kansas, to take a master's degree in liberal studies. She happily reports, "I'm always satisfied when I'm in a learning situation." Nola joked with Jay Leno on The Tonight Show *that she planned to seek employment on a cruise ship as a storyteller. This woman is not wrestling with passivity.*

---

it became a part of the national lexicon, it has been brushed aside by time and misunderstanding. Co-dependency is real and one of the worst enemies of doing what you love.

So what is co-dependency? It can be stated this way— "I'm afraid to tell you what I feel, need, and even what my dreams and aspirations are because of how it might make you feel. So I won't tell you."

Co-dependency is also about making sure everyone's needs are taken care of while neglecting your own. It is an unfair, uneven exchange of energy. This is because somewhere in their lives, co-dependent people switched from a "me" to a "we" and forgot all about "Love your neighbor as you love yourself." Co-dependents give and give and get little if anything back. Mostly they give up themselves for others—and then harbor great resentment for doing so. Co-dependency is also a way people numb their own feelings. Even if you're not addicted to alcohol, drugs, work, rage, sex, or gambling, you could still be addicted to people pleasing.

Co-dependency will numb your feelings of sadness, anger, hurt, fear, or loneliness as well as any traditional medications. By focusing on someone else's feelings, dreams, disappointments, or victories, you don't have to deal with your own. When you're about to die, someone else's life flashes before your eyes. Ironically, co-dependency is in many ways a disease of selfishness. When you micromanage another's life, you don't notice how your own life has become unmanageable, your own dreams slipping through your fingers like sand. By ignoring your passions and helping others achieve theirs, you end up looking like the healthy, compassionate, intelligent, spiritual one, at least on the surface. Co-dependents are forever relying on external sources to make and keep them happy. If they have enough money they're happy, and if they don't they're unable to be calm and at peace. If their children are happy then they are happy. If their spouse is doing well then they feel they are doing well. If Mama is happy or Daddy is happy then everyone in the family is temporarily comfortable and secure.

By focusing on someone else's feelings, dreams, disappointments, or victories, you don't have to deal with your own.

Co-dependent people have little or no ability to internally create peace of mind, serenity, self-esteem, and self-worth as they focus on others. In the process they might look damn good but they're likely exhausted.

All of this leads to the undeniable fact that if you are prone to co-dependency, you must face it in order to live your dreams. You can join a self-help group, read *Codependent No More,* and even seek treatment from the few sources that still provide it. I'm a recovering co-dependent myself, and this work is some of the most rewarding I've ever done.

A big leap into the passion sea is to be able not to care too much what others think, especially those who do not support your visions of a fuller life.

Religion

Many people practice their religion in a way that literally prohibits them from seeing their own gold and letting it shine like the sun. Many fundamentalist Buddhists, Christians, Muslims or Jews—hold to the tenet that in order to truly be one of God's own, you have to suffer, do without, give everything away, negate yourself anytime you even appear to be putting yourself first and foremost.

Going back to money for a moment, some people's religious indoctrination included the teaching that somehow money is evil: "A rich man would have as much difficulty getting to heaven as a camel would crawling through an eye of a needle."

On the opposite side are those who preach humility while driving Rolls-Royces, living in palaces, and making millions of dollars from the behemoth churches and temples they erect to seat thousands.

Many of the New Age prophets of "abundance" tend to shame their followers if they have not focused their "intention" and affirmed their wealth. This leads some to feel they have done something wrong if they have not attracted abundance sufficiently.

Self-Talk

The last, but certainly not least, most commonly cited detractor is our own self-talk. This is the constantly playing tape loop in our minds that tell us things like:

"You're not smart enough."

"You are not talented enough."

"You don't deserve it."

"Shame on you for being so selfish."

"You can't have everything."

"You are not in touch with reality."

"It is impossible to capture your dream—you've always been a dreamer."

These self-defeating monologues and messages become more burdensome with time, and pretty soon we begin to believe them. This is usually because someone we respected, loved, or admired drilled them into us at a very early age. Davis's father told him he was "retarded" all his childhood. Although Davis went on from college to earn a master's degree in physics and a doctorate in chemistry, at forty-three he still lives with the suspicion that he was mentally challenged. He subsists as a researcher when his dream is to teach college. What self-defeating messages were you given as a child or young adult that still cling to your brain and being?

OVERCOMING THE FIVE GREAT FEARS

Let's stay with our old friend fear for just a few more minutes. In the Buddhist tradition they say there are five great fears that stand between us and freedom:

- Fear of losing our livelihood
- Fear of losing our life
- Fear of losing our reputation
- Fear of losing our mind
- Fear of speaking our truths in public

Fear of Losing Our Livelihood

The loss of our livelihood is one of the greatest fears that most people will ever conquer. If the Buddhists are right, if we do not conquer this fear in this lifetime we will come back and get another opportunity. If the Baptists are right, we only get this one shot, so we'd better get busy. More people than I care to remember have said to me, "I can't quit the job I have. What if I don't get another one?"

This is similar to another refrain: "I can't leave this person. I'll never find anyone who loves me as much." But remember losing your high school sweetheart and thinking you would never love again? Remember breaking up with the college "love of your life" and thinking there would never be another? Remember divorcing your first spouse and thinking ... Well, you get the picture. It's the same with jobs, even in a slumping economy. But this fear is so set into us at a cellular level that it's hard to shake out of our bones.

Fear of Losing Our Life

Loss of life is another great fear. Losing our job, spouse, health, insurance, pension, or retirement may lead us to feel like death is on our heels, stalking us, just waiting for the right moment to strike. We even say things like, "If she leaves me, it will kill me," or "I'll die if I lose this job."

When the Buddha was a boy, it was prophesied that should he see "death," he would leave his father's luxurious palace of plenty. So his father tried to shield his son Siddhartha from such a troublesome sight. Once he saw the Grim Reaper's handiwork, however, he began his journey toward enlightenment.

Fear of Losing Our Reputation

I don't know about where you live, but here in the South we are taught to protect our reputations at all costs. A girl's reputation is to remain untarnished. Parents' reputations within their communities are sacrosanct, not to be defiled by some wayward child's bad behaviors or airing of the family's dirty laundry. When I was a boy, a divorced woman might as well have had a scarlet A pinned to her jumpsuit, and while this has changed some in large cities, in small towns and communities—not so much. Bankruptcy was virtually unheard of, and paying your bills even a day late brought disgrace and shame upon the family name. Going back on your word after sealing a deal with a handshake was downright evil.

Fear of Losing Our Mind

Fear that we may have gone around the bend can be terrifying. A client I'll call Bob wanted with all his heart and soul to join the Peace Corps back in the early 1970s. He was a trust-fund baby from a very prominent family on Long Island. After graduating from Columbia University, he told his family his plans. The first thing out of his father's mouth was, "You must be out of your mind!" His aunts and uncles, cousins, and society friends all told him he was "crazy" to give up his comforts and go help the underprivileged. Even today when we have a session, he often begins talking about whatever is bothering him with the phrase, "You're probably going to think I'm nuts," or "Tell me if you think I'm going crazy." This fear infiltrated into his psyche early, and still keeps him from doing what he loves, going into the Peace Corps at fifty.

See if any of these phrases rings a bell—maybe you've uttered them, or perhaps someone else has said them to you at some point in life:

"You'd be out of your mind to quit such a good job with benefits."

"You are crazy to be thinking about going to college at your age."

"Are you insane?"

"You must be losing your mind."

"My ex-wife/husband is nuts."

"You need professional help."

The fear of losing our mind or having people think we have "lost it" or "gone off the deep end" is so prevalent that many, many people have stayed in dead-end marriages, unsatisfying jobs, and much more to keep it at bay.

Fear of Speaking Our Truths in Public

The final fear in the Buddhist's list is fear of speaking our minds in public. This is closely akin to the fear of being thought crazy. However, speaking our truths to loved ones or strangers, friends, and colleagues, is terrifying for most people, so we designate a handful of people to do it for us—Martin Luther King, Abraham Lincoln, Gandhi, Jesus, John and Robert Kennedy—and look where it got them. Is it any wonder it brings up such terror in us tenuous souls?

If speaking our truths doesn't get us killed, it certainly has caused many to lose their livelihoods, marriages, and reputations. And yet to follow our passions, dreams, or bliss often requires that we push through all these various and sundry fears.

STOPPING THE LYING

There is a running joke in Alcoholics Anonymous: "How do you know if an alcoholic is lying?" Answer: "Is his mouth moving?" Many of you lie to yourselves and to others much more than you would really like to, and much more than necessary. One of the most recognizable traits of adult children from dysfunctional families is that we lie when it would be just as easy to tell the truth. Lying is that deeply ingrained. Lying is also one of the great behaviors passive people regularly employ. Why do we do this? One answer is found in the

Lies temporarily keep us from feeling our feelings, especially anger and sadness.

purpose of the lies. Lying is designed to let us avoid actions we don't want to take but are too passive, co-dependent, and people pleasing to just say no to outright. Lies are the "I'll call in sick" cards we play to avoid confrontation at work or the "tell them I'm not here" responses when the phone rings. Lies temporarily keep us from feeling our feelings, especially anger and sadness. Each of these lies leads to passivity, and passivity produces more and more lies.

Listen long enough to the lies you tell yourself and others and you'll start believing them . . . until you find yourself stagnant and not moving toward your true self at all. We become depressed and tell ourselves more lies about our depression:

It's hopeless and forever so what's the use of movement or action? This sort of avoidance thus keeps at bay one of the keys to coming out of passivity.

As Steve Chandler says in his book *17 Lies That Are Holding You Back & the Truth That Will Set You Free*, "As adults we have talked ourselves into a conspiracy of frozen living. The lies we tell justify the deep freeze we are in, the paralyzed existence. The lies justify and explain why we are always so stuck."

It really is the truth that will set us free. Janet, a forty-two-year-old Harvard graduate, runs her own clothing store chain. Everyone she knows has heard her describe how unhappy she is in her marriage. Her husband is a head football coach at the university near their home. She always makes it clear that he is not mean to her, never hits, doesn't have a drinking problem—but he just isn't ever there for her emotionally, sexually, intellectually, or spiritually. Year after year she says she wants out.

She came to see me on the recommendation of her therapist, who had heard this message from her once a week for years. The first thing out of her mouth when I asked her why she came was, "I am miserable in my marriage and I want out. I want to live a fuller, richer life with a man who is really present and attentive."

I told her, "No, you don't want out, and that is the truth. If you can fully embrace this truth as the foundation from which to build a strategy, then you are halfway out of the relationship that causes you so much pain. If you keep thinking and telling yourself, your friends, your therapist, and me that you want out and keep this illusion in place, you will still be in the same place ten years from now. However, if you will accept the reality that you really don't want out and make a list of reasons why you're staying—then and only then can you really be free to leave this relationship."

She looked at me with anger, then comprehension in her eyes. "I thought you would just listen to me like everybody else does, but what you said is true. Why hasn't my therapist pointed this out to me before?"

Janet's question, "Why didn't my therapist point this out before . . . ?" has been asked by hundreds of people over the years that I have been coaching and counseling.

Straight talk therapy can indeed further promote passivity. Think about it. The therapist trained in this modality sits and listens and says, "Uh-huh, tell me more." Now, obviously I'm overstating this to make a point, but in truth not only is the body *not* engaged, but more often than not the emotions are just as absent from a session. The spirit and soul of the client remain hidden behind a barrage of words; the few intellectual insights that are gained are often forgotten twenty minutes after the session is over.

Dialogue Between Faith and Fear

Still unsure you can push through your various fears and do what you most love? Then let's do another exercise. This one is called the Dialogue Between Faith and Fear.

Fear	Faith
• *Wait until the economy gets better.*	• *Listen to my heart now.*
• *Be realistic.*	• *Dreams can be real.*
• *Wait until I retire; then I can do whatever I want.*	• *The time is now.*
• *This is my lot in life.*	• *I am the captain of this ship.*

The Five-Question Reality Test

1. *What do I get from staying where I am?*
2. *What do I not have to do?*
3. *What are my true fears that I don't have to face?*
4. *What do I get from parents, family, friends, and therapist by not changing?*
5. *Who have I seen modeling the behaviors that I am exhibiting?*

Solving the Abandonment Problem That Leads to Passivity

Not everyone reading this book was abandoned. But unfortunately, many of you were. One thing I know for sure after working with thousands of people over the years is that it will be very difficult to remember who you wanted to be if you do not delve deeply into the pain of abandonment. And remember that if you were smothered, you were also abandoned, just in a different way. Many of you were not maliciously or intentionally abandoned, but you still need to acknowledge it.

Babies are born dependent, literally connected to Mom and figuratively to Dad. When the umbilical cord is cut and the infant breathes in that first breath, the baby's being becomes a space to be filled with the special energies we call love, presence, attention, and time. If you were raised by parents who did not themselves receive an abundance of these things, then it may be that they could only give so much to you. This can be and should be seen as the original or primal trauma. Some parents actually take their children's energy to fill their own empty spaces, which consistently leaves the child feeling abandoned. This is a form of abandonment that is seldom dealt with but forever played out. The child (and later adult) comes to associate feeling drained and left with love, leading him or her to assume that this is what a committed relationship is.

Many of you were not maliciously or intentionally abandoned, but you still need to acknowledge it.

Edrita Fried says, "Patients who lacked the good fortune of mothers in tune with their needs, who did not grow up in a family that upheld and sustained the child—'a good holding environment,' as it has been called—become obsessed with desertion." They are constantly and consistently setting up the scenarios of leaving or being left. They unconsciously pick loved ones who are certain to leave them; if they don't, then the passive people will push the loved ones out the door—and oftentimes not so gently.

Repeatedly I hear people say, "I keep picking the same man or woman over and over." This pattern, termed repetition compulsion by Freud, is an attempt to modify or reduce the aftereffects of the original trauma. By repeating the same types of relationships suffered while in a helpless, passive state (most often childhood), we are actually trying to become master of our fate. However, what tends to happen is the living definition of insanity, doing the same thing over and over and expecting different results.

The Anger Solution to Abandonment

Writers of academic texts agree that one of the main ways to treat passivity is anger work. As Dr. Edrita Fried says in *Active/Passive*, anger work can offer "escape routes from inertia to activeness." Fried goes on to note that the expression of anger and rage leads to self-understanding and insight, both necessary prerequisites to coming out of passivity.

When I ask clients or workshop participants whom they are most angry at, 80 to 90 percent declare it to be themselves. In other words, anger is turned inward again and again. It doesn't take long for these people to become de-energized, eventually depressed, and ultimately passive. If we are angry at ourselves, then we can easily engage in all kinds of self-sabotaging behaviors. If we are angry at ourselves, then failure becomes the punishment we feel we deserve. Turning this emotion inward does nothing constructive. Anger expressed appropriately and directed at the proper sources, on the other hand, gets us out of stuck places like passivity.

If we are angry at ourselves, then failure becomes the punishment we feel we deserve.

In order to express anger appropriately, many people first have to come to understand the differences between holding someone or some institution accountable and blaming them. Then the difference between *accountable* and *responsible* must be clear.

The Difference Between Accountability and Blaming

Blame is about self-pity and being a victim. Accountability is taking action and expressing your thoughts, feelings, and emotions for the way you have been treated, hurt, wounded, traumatized, or simply let down and disappointed.

Blame creates distance, hurts everyone, and accomplishes nothing. Judson said in a session with me, "My mother's disappearance when I was six made me the man I am today. Everything I do or say or don't do or say is so I won't get left again." Writing a letter of accountability hurts no one. Telling your therapist how your father emotionally beat you down and taught you to beat down your son is more likely to motivate you to stop abusing your children. Admitting to a counselor or a trusted confidant that your parents, schools, churches, or synagogues taught you little or nothing about how to have mature relationships humbles you enough to take responsibility to learn. Getting angry with who or what is accountable will get people out of stuck places and into the flow of a healthy life.

Blame creates distance, hurts everyone, and accomplishes nothing.

Recently I was working with a woman who "never finishes anything." When we went back into her past, one of her first memories was of swimming competitively at six years old. She loved it. She then told of having to practice in an unheated pool in the wintertime; when she told the coach it was too cold, he pushed her small body in anyway. She quit swimming that day and became "angry at myself for never finishing anything. Now I realize I am angry at him and have been for years but always repressed it until now." The poet Rainer Maria Rilke says, "The abused becomes the abuser."

Assigning Accountability and Taking Responsibility

Even highly educated people tend to confuse words and use them interchangeably. *Accountability* and *responsibility* are good examples. Unfortunately, many well-intentioned therapists, priests, and sponsors misunderstand these two incredibly powerful and potent words, telling their listeners that they are accountable when they should say responsible and responsible when they mean accountable. Webster's defines *accountability* as "liable to pay or make good in case of loss." *Responsibility,* says the dictionary, is being "able to respond to any claim."

Let me give an example. I am driving down the road at the speed limit and I come to an intersection where I have a green light. I proceed through the intersection, and the driver of another car zooms through his red light and hits me. Who is accountable? The red-light runner—that's who. I'm going to get out of my car, shaken up a bit, probably a little scared and probably a little angry if I'm not too much in shock (which I'll say much more about later), and ask him if he has insurance to pay for my damaged car. I will hold him "accountable." Then I'll be "responsible" and take my car to the body shop to have it repaired. If I hold myself accountable for the other person running the red light, I'll tell myself it was my fault for being in the wrong place at the wrong time and tell the red-light runner, "Oh, I'm so sorry I got in your line of fire. How silly that was of me to think I could drive down the road expecting others to obey the law. It's not necessary to contact your insurance agent, I'll pay for the damages—mine and yours—have a good day." Equally ridiculous would be something like, "Look, you red-light runner, you come by my house tomorrow and pick up my damaged car and take it to the body shop, then go back and pick it up when they're done and bring it to me. In the meantime give me the keys to your wife's car; I'll be driving it until you get mine fixed." You ran into me, so you are accountable. I'll take the car to be fixed—I'm responsible for getting the repairs done.

If you carry both the weight of accountability and the weight of responsibility, the two together will weigh you down so much you'll be exhausted and probably not have enough strength to handle both. You'll probably slip even deeper into passivity. Most of the men and women I have worked with, myself included, believed as children that we were the reasons why our father or mother drank, fought with each other, or abused us. I've heard hundreds say, "I probably deserved it. I was always getting into some kind of trouble." We make ourselves both accountable and responsible for their behavior. Even if we were ignored, left, or smothered, we assigned ourselves accountability from childhood on.

What I suggest to my clients and workshop participants is to assign accountability and take responsibility. Most of the time this is done in the form of writing a letter that we do not send, fantasy dialoguing, sharing with a therapist, storytelling, creating, and the like. You do not have to actually confront other people to hold them accountable.

Assign accountability and take responsibility.

Here is another example. When Stacy went to college at seventeen, it didn't take her long to realize she had not been prepared for college-level work. She remembers thinking that she was "stupid," "dumb," "ignorant," and "illiterate." She was angry with herself for being this way. It took her a long time to shake these labels. Although she had a slightly above-average IQ, the public schools she attended in Alabama were well below the national average in literacy. After many years of being angry with herself, she realized through much hard work that the schools and teachers were accountable to teach, and she was responsible to learn. "While there were a few good teachers, there were many more who pushed us from grade to grade to get rid of us and make room for others coming in," she said. She felt her school was more like a daycare center for career juvenile delinquents who smashed more than a few streetlamps and smoked behind the gym. Finally, she felt her anger at the educational system that rolled her out on their conveyor belt before they'd tightened all her bolts and double-checked her intellectual and scholastic engine. Then she had to become responsible for doing something about it, which in her case meant learning what she should have been taught in junior high and high school. She had to study three times as hard as her fellow students who lived in school districts that held their teachers accountable for teaching the proper information and dispensing a reasonable education. But she did so.

There are those who are angry with themselves for being fifty years old without knowing "how to do a relationship," as if they were supposed to be born with this knowledge. We do, we repeat, we parrot what was shown to us and what was taught to us. If that modeling was poor, we need to transfer the weight of holding ourselves accountable, get angry, and then get responsible for educating ourselves.

Anger is a feeling that is meant to circulate like a spring. As long as that anger is about current injustices, slights, wrongs, hurts, rejections, or slanders, it will flow up and out into the world as it should, rather than down and back into our bodies, where it stagnates. If it's employed and expressed appropriately, anger can be used to get individuals, couples, families, corporations, and nations out of the stuck, dead-end, passive places.

Anger is a feeling that is meant to circulate like a spring.

Rosa Parks's anger in 1955 is what contributed to her and a whole race of people no longer being stuck at the back of the bus. Anger is what got our country out of Vietnam. Anger can move a person out of abusive relationships. The women's movement was fueled by an anger that was long overdue. The outcome forever changed the world we live in for the better.

Why Everyone Tries to Avoid Anger

One of the reasons so many of us feel uncomfortable employing anger to get out of our passivity is that we've been taught and threatened with the belief that anger is bad, negative, uncivilized, rude, and unacceptable. Add these to the misinformation and misconceptions that anger leads to more anger and that expressing anger increases blood pressure and heart problems, and it is no wonder we are racked with guilt and shame and increasingly tamp down and numb our emotions.

Everyone from parents to teachers and pastors has for generations been telling children things like, "Good girls and boys don't get angry." Girls have been told they are bitches, ball busters, nags, hags, and witches if they get angry. Boys have been taught to think of "angry" women that way.

People of all educational backgrounds, incomes, religious persuasions, and inclinations have it in their heads, hearts, or rear ends that anger equals pain.

When someone got angry in our childhood, we felt the slaps, hits, silent treatment, and icy stares. We were punished by being sent to bed without supper or exiled to our bedrooms or boarding schools. In other words, when someone got angry, someone got hurt.

Somewhere in our subconscious we decided early on that if anger equals pain, then the best way to keep from causing others pain or feeling pain ourselves would be to bust a gut, get a migraine, numb our bodies and souls, and just try with all our might never to get angry.

How's That Working for You?

In my experience, not well.

Most human beings get mildly or massively angry every twenty-four to forty-eight hours, or at the very least once a week. Yes, even nice people.

Here's the problem: Healthy, constructive anger has not, will not, and cannot cause pain; quite the opposite. If anger is expressed appropriately, it equals energy, intimacy, peace of mind, and an end to passive behavior. I'll say more on this later. For now, what you need to know is that it is unhealthy, destructive anger that causes everyone pain. The one experiencing and expressing destructive anger and all those within the vicinity of this contagious behavior are going to feel small or serious amounts of pain. In order to get a grip on rage, you need to know what it is.

RAGE AS A FORM OF PASSIVITY

Pain, violence, and punishment have nothing to do with constructive anger and everything to do with destructive anger—which is really a poor disguise for rage.

Rage is as different from anger as night is from day; as apples are from orangutans. Remember, anger is a feeling and emotion.

Rage is an action or behavior used to disconnect us from any and all emotions. Rage numbs people's feelings.

Rage is an action or behavior used to disconnect us from any and all emotions.

Cocaine, alcohol, heroin, and sugar numb us. Too much of anything numbs us, in fact—too much television, too much time at the computer or at work; all ways to numb our feelings.

Rage is like a huge dose of morphine. But it is a drug that is legal, plentiful, readily available, and can be addictive.

Rage creates more rage. It is more contagious than the flu. Rage spreads like the wildfires in California, destroying everything and everyone in its path. It is a huge factor in divorces, and dissolution of families, friendships, and business partnerships.

At fifty years old Burt is prematurely gray, but his face and body look like they belong to a man half his age. In my consultations with him he discovered—as many men I've worked with have—that when his building company business is bad, he rages at his employees and even his own family members (especially his brother, his on-site foreman) rather than feeling afraid or like a failure, or taking constructive action. On the surface Burt's rage looks more potent and powerful than being a scared businessman who shakes in fear when viewing the bottom line. To Burt, rage feels temporarily empowering, but here's the rub: It is only an illusion. Rage weakens both the rager and the one who takes the brunt of the rage. The end result is that passivity plagues both.

Lindsey an attractive stay-at-home mom, is sad and lonely most of the time because she is married to a workaholic, alcoholic husband. He is rarely home, and when he is, he's unbearable. Lindsey refuses to sleep in the same bed with him, and her retail therapy binges have maxed out their credit cards. Is this healthy anger? No—Lindsey's actions are examples of rage. When I asked her if it was time she felt her anger and extricated herself from this painful, passive partnership, she responded, "How can I get angry at him? He works hard for us, and his drinking isn't really that bad." She could not see how her rage was throwing them both into financial, not to mention emotional, ruin, and she was in denial about having any anger, healthy or unhealthy.

Rage weakens both the rager and the one who takes the brunt of the rage.

If destructive anger is identified and understood, seen for what it is, and dealt with, all kinds of feelings, emotions, memories, hurts, slights, abandonments, and other issues that have been locked inside (perhaps for decades) will surface.

How to Tell the Difference Between Anger and Rage

Anger is about the here and now; it is an active response to issues and situations occurring at the present time. You feel anger because of what your boss said to you this morning or because your spouse incorrectly balanced the checkbook this week.

Rage is about the there and then; it is about the past. Rage is a reaction to what your boss has said to you every morning for the last year. What you've stuffed and bottled up all this time suddenly gushes out like a geyser. Likewise, rage occurs because the checkbook has gone unbalanced for two years, seemingly warranting a deafening silence to correct or punish your spouse's behavior.

Because anger lives in the now, it takes moments or minutes at the most to be felt and expressed. When Jerome's wife was late for a special luncheon they'd planned, Jerome said, "I'm angry. Now I only have forty-five minutes left for lunch before I have to return for work. Let's eat and make the most of our time."

Rage, on the other hand, can take a very long time to surface because it is grounded in our personal life history. Mary Ellen's now ex-boyfriend was chronically late. She finally let loose with rage: "I'm tired of you always putting everything before me. Didn't your mother teach you it is rude to keep people waiting? I got here on time. I can't see why you can't!" . . . and she was just getting warmed up. Clearly, there was more than anger going on.

Rage is what constitutes most marathon arguments. You know, the ones that begin after the kids are put to bed and

What Is Healthy Anger?	What Is Rage/Unhealthy Anger?
• *A feeling*	• *Stuffing or masking emotions*
• *Expressing a primary emotion*	• *Negative and inappropriate*
• *Neither positive nor negative*	• *Exhausting*
• *Energizing*	• *Kept bottled up or explodes*
• *Meant to be expressed*	• *Hurts everyone involved*
• *Doesn't hurt anyone*	• *Clouds communication*
• *Clears the air*	• *Adds to confusion*
• *Increases understanding*	• *Increases conflicts and misunderstandings*
• *Helps communication*	• *Is itself an injustice and wrongs people further*
• *Rights injustices and wrongs*	• *Decreases energy, increases the distance between people, and causes discord*
• *Increases energy, intimacy, and peace of mind*	• *Damaging*
• *Healing*	• *Pervasive, out of control, and misdirected*
• *Contained and controlled until expressed at proper time, place, and person*	• *About the past*
• *About the present*	• *About "you"*
• *About "me"*	
• *A reaction*	

are still going strong at one in the morning. They end when someone cries "uncle" or attempts to just share some feelings.

Anger is about me, and rage is about you. If I express anger, I am telling you about me. Anger is revealing. If I am raging, I'm concealing what I'm really feeling and going through.

Anger is about me, and rage is about you.

Instead, rage is about other people: what they didn't do and shouldn't have done; why what they said is wrong, crazy, sick, and messed up.

Rage has moved more people out of relationships than U-Haul. It shoves everyone out the door, out of lives, or out of business. Rage pushes everyone away because no one wants to be around it. On the other hand, anger expressed in present time and in an appropriate manner actually draws people to you. If a man says to his wife, "I'm angry and I need to talk," nine times out of ten the wife will respond with something like, "Okay, tell me more," or "I'm listening," or "What's going on?"

If an employee says to a fellow worker, "I'm angry about what went on in the staff meeting this morning," most fellow employees will say, "Tell me more," or "Let's talk about it this afternoon over a beer." In other words, if I do not rage at you, you have no reason to run—indeed, anger can create the beginning of many productive dialogues and initiate problem solving.

Rage engenders defensiveness, distance, and the feeling of being in some kind of danger; it shows disrespect and disregard for both the speaker and the one pretending to listen. Anger shows appreciation and respect. If a boss is angry and says so and follows that statement with something like, ". . . and I'd like for you to meet me for lunch so we can discuss the issue"—this says, *I value you and our relationship enough to make some time and request that you make some time to resolve the issue at hand.*

Rage says in no uncertain terms *I do not value you or this relationship enough to warrant an expenditure of my time or energy to try to achieve resolution.*

Anger is a response to injustice, rudeness, impoliteness, impoverishment, impudence, and abuse. Rage is a reaction to situations, circumstances, people, processes, and problems. Responses are generated by present stimuli. Reactions are a reactivation of our history and memories about people, processes, and problems.

These rage reactions are almost always disproportionate to what is being said or done or not said or done to our satisfaction. Angry responses are proportional to what is coming toward us or being taken away from us.

Rage elicits such reactions as: "Where is all of this coming from . . . ?" or "Why are you making a mountain out of a molehill?" Rage incorporates statements like *You always,* or *You never.* It often includes ultimatums and threats. The one raging holds a black-and-white mentality, all or nothing, my way or the highway. Anger uses words like *sometimes, occasionally,* and *every now and then.* Anger is comfortable with some gray areas.

Anger engages conflict, and rage runs from it. Angry men or women are in essence saying, *I have a problem and I am seeking a solution.* Rage says, *You have a problem and that's the problem—no solution in sight.*

Anger says, *Let's confront these divisive issues;* rage says, *Let's further divide.* A CEO who attended one of my corporate anger presentations stood up during my talk and said, "I never run from confrontations. I stand toe-to-toe with anyone. I get in their face no matter what I have to do or say to get my point across." The sturdy sixty-year-old with a crew cut sat down with a satisfied look on his face.

> *Anger engages conflict, and rage runs from it.*

I responded, "Does that include yelling, calling people names, and similar behaviors or actions?"

"Whatever it takes!" he replied.

The actions and behaviors often employed in conflicted situations are self-defeating. One reason is that many people (including the aforementioned CEO) are avoiding conflict, despite appearances. They hate confrontations because in the past this meant they felt defeated by their parents, coaches, teachers, or spouses.

But perhaps a more significant explanation for so much avoidance is that most people have not been taught how to

Passive Words Used by the Raging Person

You always _____.

You never _____.

Why can't you just _____.

If only you _____.

It's all your fault.

Shame on you.

You're lying.

When are you going to _____.

deal with conflict or engage in confrontation with a win–win attitude. Instead we're taught there can only be one winner or one loser—an approach grounded in rage.

When we realize that inappropriate actions and reactions such as rage cover our emotions, we are granted a new freedom to speak our feelings without fear of retaliation and retribution. Once our responses are proportional to people and circumstances, neither the speaker nor listener has anything to fear.

GRIEVING: A FOUR-STEP MODEL TO TREAT ABANDONMENT

Let's be clear. When a man, woman, or child is crying, it is because a hurt has already occurred. Crying or grieving is part of the process of healing the hurt that comes from being abandoned.

Many men and women fear sadness and grief. They're afraid that if they succumb to their sorrows, then the black dog—depression—will devour their minds and souls. This fear is strengthened because they have confused grief with self-pity. The latter, if given time, will turn into depression and passivity.

How do you start grieving, having been abandoned or smothered? What does it look like, sound like, and feel like? Grieving is different for everyone, but the process described below generally holds true for most.

Step 1. Recognize the Need to Grieve.

The first thing you must do is to become conscious of the necessity to grieve all your losses of any kind, no matter how big or small and no matter what anybody tells you or thinks. You must completely reject the toxic teachings that have become worn-out clichés when it comes to genuine grief work: It's just water under the bridge, let sleeping dogs lie, no use in crying over spilt milk, get over it, get back in the saddle, pull yourself up by the bootstraps, keep a stiff upper lip, the past is dead and gone. As William Faulkner, the great Southern writer, said, "The past isn't dead; it's not even the past."

You need to not only mourn the loss of things, people, places, pets, stages, transitions, and changes, but also the things, people, pets, and so forth that you wanted but never got. Not having is also a loss to be mourned. However, having been abandoned—whether for minutes, months, or years—is one of the greatest losses that grieving can heal.

Not having is also a loss to be mourned.

Tony is a data entry processor who told me how his mother married for the second time and had a child with his stepfather. She then devoted all her attention, support, and nurturing toward his half brother. "She always took his side," he went on to say; "even on her deathbed she wanted him there and not me. She even refused to tell me anything about my real father." You can see clearly how James experienced abandonment.

Step 2. Get a Support Network.

You'll want to develop a support network of people who will stand by you while you're doing your grieving. This might include friends, family, therapist, God or Higher Power, sponsor, or all of the above—the more the better. These are people who will not hurry you, shame you, or talk you out of your grief. This group shows you, *We're here and we know grieving can be scary—that's why you shouldn't do it alone. Indeed, you have been alone long enough.* In other words, use your community to hold your hand while you walk through what can feel like the "valley of the shadow of death."

Many of us have been told not to show our feelings and thus believe that grief should be a solitary act, if it's an act at all. But grieving was never meant to be done entirely alone. There is a tribe in the Polynesian islands that provides the best example of how grieving is a community task. When someone in the immediate family dies, it is everyone's job to mourn and grieve the loss for a full year. During that time tribe members take care of the children, the garden, the home, the cooking, and the cleaning for the grievers. At the end of the year, the grief cycle is completed and worked through because that was their sole/soul focus. The family then resumes the business of life.

Step 3. Create a Grief Ritual.

The only person who will know when you are done grieving is you. But it's important to make the time to grieve. For example, it may be necessary to set aside time each day or once a week or whatever is appropriate for you. You might get up thirty minutes early before going to work and take out a picture of the person who left you, light some candles, and look at the photograph. Tell the person how you feel, what you loved and hated about them, and then weep, wail, get angry—whatever gives a voice to your abandoned self. Then get up, take a shower, and go to work.

Remember, a ritual is something you do over and over again until it is no longer necessary.

Remember, a ritual is something you do over and over again until it is no longer necessary. Some last for weeks, months, years, or lifetimes. Grief rituals usually take six months to a year. What most people do, if they do anything at all, is what I call hit-or-miss grieving. They will a do a lot of grief work on having been abandoned for a day or two or a week and convince themselves they are finished. Or perhaps some idiot—sometimes their own therapist or sponsor—tells them they "should be done" and move on. Give yourself time.

Step 4. Celebrate.

I've found it important to have a ceremony at the end of your grieving process. This can be done by, say, inviting the friends who stood by you to someplace special—your favorite restaurant or park—thanking them for the support they gave, and letting them and you see that you navigated the treacherous waters in your body's ocean of grief. Do you remember Alice in Wonderland? The only way she could get through the huge locked door was to cry and cry. Pretty soon she raised herself on a river of her own tears and floated right through the keyhole to the other side of the door—and the other side of her life.

How will you know when it's time for the ceremony? You'll be in a place to celebrate and see more of the positive sides of the person or people who have left you. You'll be able to praise them and yourself for all the gifts you gave each other and all the lessons you learned. You will be able to express a measure of gratitude for the time you spent in whatever relationship it was that's now over, and there will be no residual grief, anger, or resentment. You will bless the person who left you and became the catalyst for change; ultimately you might even be able to totally forgive. These are all signs that you have successfully come through this painful period in your healing journey. However, if you find yourself telling the bartender what a shitty father/mother/priest you had . . . you're probably not done. Go back to step 1.

How will you know when it's time for the ceremony? You'll be in a place to celebrate.

At a workshop on grief and abandonment, a man asked me the question, "What do you do if you didn't make time to grieve the fact and feeling that you were abandoned but you're already in another relationship? Won't it upset my partner to see me grieving?" The short answer is no. Emotionally intelligent partners tend to know if their loved one has been abandoned and if that wound has been healed deeply or not. These healthy partners will give you time and support to get the past out of your body, dreams, nightmares, and souls: It will make room in their hearts for the present person they love and cherish. Once you've fully grieved, they will no longer always fear being left, and the current relationship will be a healthier one.

Working with Abandonment Issues in Therapy

Unfortunately, abandonment is most often treated by therapists as a symptom rather than as a core issue that has shaped the client's life since early childhood. Often a therapist, counselor, or psychologist will let adult clients go on for hours about how their spouse "abandoned" them for another lover, or for work. But that therapist will not take them back to the original abandonment incidents for several reasons:

- Most therapists have not worked significantly on their own abandonment issues.

- The overwhelming number of therapists practicing today still rely on "talk therapy" to deal with every kind of issue. However, core abandonment or original trauma is not remembered and held in the minds of those who experienced it from birth through age six and thus can almost never be successfully "talked out."

- Memory of abandonment is stored at a cellular, bone, belly, butt, tissue level and therefore must be accessed from those areas and released. We know this because when people experience present-time loss and the feelings that come from being left, they often have somatic complaints—fever, chills, vomiting, nausea, cramping, sweating, heart palpitations, diarrhea, and others—that last for hours, days, weeks, even months after they know they "should be over it by now." Most practicing therapists do not implement this "body-centered" approach due to either lack of training or lack of confidence in its effectiveness. Some of those who might be open to it do not have the space necessary to facilitate the intense emotional expressions that need to come forth and be fully expressed. In addition, the fifty-minute hour does not leave adequate time for clients to feel safe delving into their bodies and connecting with the pain of abandonment—they know that no sooner than they do so, it will be time to pull back out and repress any emotion that might have been available.

Examples of Body-Centered Therapy

Many who practice body-centered therapy do so in an hour-and-a-half or longer format, giving clients the chance to feel safe knowing they have adequate time to feel all their emotions. Most practioners are comfortable with the clients' anger, rage, fear, and grief and know how to facilitate the release of these powerful emotions. A few examples follow.

Brett was forty-four years old, a good-looking slender man who was a gourmet chef. He had been in a number of relationships but was compelled to avoid marriage. He went from woman to woman; whenever one got serious, he would fly away. He identified deeply with my first book, *The Flying Boy: Healing the Wounded Man.* One night during a men's group that I led at the Austin Men's Center (a holistic facility I founded in 1987), he mentioned that he was feeling very lonely but just plain couldn't figure out why he had such an aversion to marriage.

I had him lie down on the carpeted floor of a room almost barren except for overstuffed pillows, boxes of tissues, plastic bats, old tennis rackets, and twelve other men. I asked him to take deep full breaths. After five or six minutes, I gave him a prompting phrase—*Please don't go*—and encouraged him to modify it to more accurately articulate his feelings. He repeated the phrase several times, and then tears started slowly forming and flowing down his face. He repeated it a few more times, then changed it to *How could you take her away and not let me say good-bye?* He repeated this phrase several times, each time descending farther into his body and farther into his past. He just kept repeating the phrase and sobbing for about ten more minutes. Then he started talking about an incident he had been storing in his body for four decades. It went back to kindergarten, where he had his first best friend, a little girl. They played together, took naps together, drew and painted together, and visited each other when school was out because she lived only two houses down. Weeping, he told the story of how one day he went to school and she wasn't there. Her family had moved without letting the two children say good-bye. When he started crying, the teacher scolded him and shamed him in front of the class. Some forty years later he was sobbing again, saying, "I never got to tell her good-bye." Finally, after about twenty-five minutes, he looked at me and the other men and said, "Can I really be this upset about something that happened in kindergarten? Do you think my feeling that people are going to always be taken away without so much as a good-bye has kept me from really letting any woman get close?"

One year later Brett was happily married—and he still is. Is that a coincidence? I don't think so. Do you?

～

A couple of years ago, I was facilitating a men's retreat in North Carolina. The men had built a large, warm fire in the center of the circle we had made. There were about fifty guys of all ages and backgrounds. One was in his early thirties, rugged, slim, and with a piercing look in his eyes, but he spoke almost in hushed tones. I had to ask him to speak up several times as he stood on the other side of the fire from me, asking to work on a particular issue. He began to explain: "My wife and I have tried everything to have a baby and nothing is working. I've been checked and my sperm count is fine; she has been thoroughly examined. The doctors cannot find anything that should be keeping us from conceiving. I think there is something inside me that isn't about the physical, but I have no idea what it could be." Jeremy began to fight back the tears as he spoke.

"Are you afraid of being a father?" I asked. "I sure was at your age."

"I'm afraid I will be the kind of father that my dad was, I guess."

"What kind was that?"

"The kind that left us when I was thirteen and I've never seen since. I don't want to ever do that to my kid, but there is something in me that thinks I might. In a way I keep waiting for him to come back and tell me why he left. The only thing I have of his is this baseball cap he gave me when I was twelve." He pulled the hat off and held it out, looking at it like it was pure gold. "I wear it all the time," he said.

"It would be very difficult and scary for a twelve-year-old to father a child and not be afraid that he might leave it, don't you think?" I asked.

"But I'm thirty-three. I'm not twelve."

"You are a man wearing a boy's hat, waiting for a father to come back and show you how to be a father. I'm going to make what we call down South an outlandish suggestion. Just

watch what feelings and thoughts come to you when I say it."
I paused.

"He's not coming back, is he?"

"No, I'm sad to say. And even if he did, the time for him to be a father to you has passed. It is time you become a father. It is time to feel the pain of abandonment."

"Okay. I'm ready," he said haltingly.

"I want you to take that hat off your head again, throw it into the fire, and say, *You left me but I'm not you.*"

He looked at me, and then at all the men, and then down at his hat. "What good will that do? It is the only thing I have of his." He finally let out a couple of gallons of tears.

"I honestly don't know if it will do any good. It's just a suggestion; don't do it unless you feel it's right. But although a boy can't father a child, a strong, intelligent, creative, potent man will be a damn good father because you aren't anything like your dad. Your dad wouldn't be here on his best day doing the kind of work you have committed to doing for yourself and the sake of your family."

He looked at his hat for several minutes. Then he said loudly—so loudly that everyone could hear him, maybe even his father wherever he was—"I'm not you. I won't abandon my family no matter what. You missed knowing me and I'm a damn good man." With that he threw the hat in the fire. The men gave him a standing ovation.

One year later I met with the same group of men for another workshop. Jeremy came up to me, pulled out his wallet, and showed me about a dozen pictures of his gorgeous three-month-old son.

Now for the Good News About Abandonment

If you delve deeply into your own abandonment issues—or pass this information on to someone you care about who has been abandoned—and you get angry, grieve, and let out all the sadness that comes from being left at an early age, then the only person who can ever abandon you again is you. This changes everything. You are able to come out of your passivity because you are able to engage life, people, work, relationships, parenting, and much more without the fear of being left again. Now should your lover leave, you will grieve and perhaps get angry—but it will not feel like the end of the world. Your grief, sadness, and anger at your loss will be manageable, not overwhelming. You will find that you did not give up all your power and mangle your personality out of fear they would leave if you didn't. You will be able to speak your mind, not in a callous or cold way but in a conscious and consistent manner, to your spouse, friend, boss, adult child, or colleague.

The only person who can ever abandon you again is you.

Above all, you will come to know in your body, cells, tissue, bones, belly, heart, and soul that adults cannot be abandoned—and that will bring you a deep peace. Many people never know this, instead going through life shape-shifting into myriad different forms and trying to please everyone, only to never feel really understood or known by anyone.

ACTIVE LOVING AS A SOLUTION TO PASSIVITY

Now that you no longer fear abandonment by others, you are really ready to actively give and receive love in ways you may have only dreamed about.

"Honey, do you love me?" is one of the most oft-spoken and most passive phrases anyone can say. I propose that a proper, not angry response might be, "My dear, what business is that of yours?" When I have suggested this, most people look at me like, as we say down here in the South, "a tree fell on me." Very often someone will say, "Of course it's my business. After all, we're in this relationship together."

My response comes in response to years of therapists and self-help books telling us that problems or conflicts in a relationship are 50–50. They purport that if we own up to half the issue and our partner does as well, things work out. In reality, this further aggravates latent passivity in both parties. Active loving requires 100–100. I'm 100 percent responsible for my issues, my pain, and my part in the problem we're having;

you are 100 percent responsible for your pain, your past, and your part of the problem. Now we are talking.

"Do you love me" is not only passive, it's infantile. Every child on the planet has a right and need to ask the questions,

The active or mature lover's question should be, "How well am I loving you?" "Daddy, do you love me?" or "Mama, do you love me?" Each child should receive the greatest answer: "Yes." However, the active or mature lover's question should be, "How well am I loving you?" This doesn't apply only to spouses; in any adult relationship, we should ask ourselves, *How well am I loving my son, mom, sister, friend—even God?*

So how do we develop active love rather than the passive love most of us have been taught?

The Platinum Rule of Active Loving

Nearly everyone reading this right now, religious or not, knows the golden rule—*Do unto others as you would have them do unto you.* Right? But it does not have to be followed literally. Perhaps a more helpful rule is *Do unto others the way they have been longing for probably their whole life.* When it comes to real loving relationships among spouses, lovers, families, and friends, think of *them* first. I love sports-related gifts, for instance, but if I give my wife sports-related gifts I shouldn't be surprised that they don't touch her deeply.

Jerry's wife loves flowers and she gives everybody flowers, even her two best friends who are allergic. Then she wonders why they don't appreciate her efforts.

Sending the Love They Long For

Most writers of self-help, personal-growth books fill them with their clients' case histories. If you've read this far, you've seen that I have used some myself. However, I often write about what will also help *me* grow and heal. I don't think there is much of a gap between us. In fact, I'm convinced that one way I can show each reader my love and respect is by being honest and forthcoming, telling you not only about you but also about me and my personal journey in the second half of my life.

I took to heart the golden rule—*do unto others as you would have them do unto you*—with my first wife. When I had to go on tour with my books, giving lectures all over the country and the world, I'd go to great lengths to find her gifts from different cities and countries. I brought them back to show her how much I missed her and thought about her, and to thank her for holding down the fort at home so I could make our living on the grueling road. Even if I was only gone for a day or two, I would stop by a florist or grocery store and pick up some flowers for her. She would look at the gift or the floral arrangement and say something like, "Well, isn't this nice? Thank you. That was sweet." But I never got the feeling that it really rang her bells with delight and deep appreciation. Still, I kept doing it and doing it and wondering why she didn't seem to really grasp my efforts, taste, and attempts to be romantic.

One day after many long months laboring to finish my fifth nonfiction book, I took the hand-typed pages wrapped in a gigantic rubber band and walked them into the bedroom where she was folding clothes. I started to say, "Before I let anyone else read this, I want you to take a look and tell me honestly what you think and make any suggestions or recommendations . . ." But she burst into tears and sobbed so sweetly for about ten minutes. Even though I was a highly trained counselor and coach, I didn't have the slightest idea what was happening. Luckily, I had just enough common sense not interrupt her crying with my questions. After about fifteen minutes she wiped the tears from her eyes, blew her nose, and said, "Right now I feel more loved by you than anytime in our relationship. The love you are showing me is what I have always wanted from you."

She paused and I knew the time was right. "Soooo, exactly what did I do?"

"I've been with you while you wrote three other books. When you finished each and every one, you immediately sent it off to your friends Robert Bly, Bill Stott, or Karen Blicher, asking for their opinions and criticism. But until now you have never asked for my input. I feel so respected by you and loved by you and grateful that you think enough of my opinion and my intelligence to let me go over the manuscript before they do."

The very next afternoon I walked in the door of our home after work and found the house filled with flowers of every kind. In the living room was a carefully wrapped present—and underneath the present was a clue as to how to find the next present. And so on. I started sobbing. The most important thing I opened that day was the two hearts that had been only receiving what we ourselves wanted to get instead of sending the kind of love both of us had separately wanted our whole lives. She wanted to be respected and have her intellect and creativity validated by the man she loved. What did I want? Flowers. I love flowers, have always loved flowers. As a child who never had his birthday celebrated with a party or gifts, I also wanted presents so that I could feel cherished and adored by those who loved me. But no one had ever given me flowers and presents.

Sadly, my wife and I later went our separate ways, but at least I'd stumbled onto this and other critical ways to show caring and love. After that experience I came to believe that most of us love others—including our own biological family members—the way we ourselves would like to be loved. I decided to try something I'd never done: to go see how my aging father wanted to be shown love and learn what it would be like if I

Most of us love others—including our own biological family members—the way we ourselves would like to be loved.

managed to love him just that way. We hadn't seen or spoken to each other in ten years. I guess the truth is we never really saw or really talked to each other during the four decades prior to our estrangement.

So I got in my car and drove over to his house as quickly as I could; I didn't want to have too much time to think about this and maybe change my mind. When I pulled into his driveway, he came out of the house tan, bare-chested, skin looking like an old saddle, eyes as blue as ever, and still tall and skinny. He met me at the car and stuck out the hand he'd been sticking out to me since I was four, when he said, "Son, you're too hold to be hugging or kissing a man." His grip was strong as a vise. Both of us smiled a tenuous smile and walked inside. I hugged my mother, whom I'd seen and talked to many times during my cold war with Dad. Even before the estrangement, whenever I'd call home and he'd answer the phone, he'd talk for less than two minutes: "How's work? How's the weather? Are you making any money? Well, here's your mother. She's dying to talk to you."

We went into the house and sat down on the couch. Mom brought glasses of sweet tea. "Mother, get me a map," he said. Mom handed him an Alabama/Georgia road map. He opened it and pointed to the highways that run from Atlanta to north Alabama. The first thing he asked me was, "What roads did you take to get here?" Well, figuratively the answer would be *Ten years, lots of therapy, a couple of failed relationships, and recovery from alcohol.* But I knew that what Dad was asking was what literal highways I had taken to get from my house to his. I told him. "Son, the next time you come to see me, take 575 and come through Decatur instead of taking 72 into Florence and you'll save at least fifteen minutes." I agreed to try it.

He pulled the living room curtain back and stared outside at the driveway. "What are you driving?"

"A Volvo."

"I don't know why you don't drive an American-made car. I wouldn't drive anything else. My Chrysler is a good car. I keep it tuned up and rotate my tires and I get pretty good gas mileage. What kind of mileage does that foreign car get?"

That was the conversation after ten years. That was about the extent of every conversation I'd ever had with him face-to-face since I left home at seventeen. What he said next was also what he'd always say at this point, when the conversation dried up. "Well, I'm going to work in my garden. Come on outside. I'd like to show it to you."

Here was the moment. It had presented itself many times. It could be, "Come on out to my toolshed, I'd like to show you my new tools," or "Let me show you my car's clean engine"— anything he loved, knew his way around, and didn't need a lot of words to talk about. I always wanted words, more words from him than he knew how to give. My mother, who loved words, raised me. She instilled in me a love of language— reading to me from the shiny blue Bible stories that came each month in the mail. I was my mother's son. My brother, Randy, and my sister, Kathy, were Dad's children—"chips off the old block," he called them. My brother worked with his hands like Dad, and Kathy had his knack with numbers. In years past when he ran out of words and wanted to take me to his world—the garden or the garage—I'd say something like, "Dad, can't you just sit and talk a little longer? I don't have much time before I have to get back to school" (or wherever I was in such a hurry to go).

"No, you and your Mama have plenty of talking to do. But I'd love to show you my garden."

This time I wanted to make things different. I stood up and said, "I'd love to. Let's go outside."

Before we reached the garden, he pointed and said, "Look at those squash. You ever seen such beautiful squash? Look at those tomatoes. I'll pick some and you can take them home with you. They taste better than those plastic things they sell in the grocery store."

And so it went for about thirty minutes. This man waxed eloquent on the mystical workings of fertilizer, what flowers to plant to keep this kind of bug off, the depth to plant that kind of seed. He even showed me how to run his rototiller. I saw how he had wanted me to love him all those years. I wanted, like my first wife, to have my intellect respected and my accomplishments validated by a man who didn't really understand what my advanced degree was, or even why I became a writer. This man wanted to be respected and cherished by a son who knew nothing about his passions—gardening, tools, and engines. We both learned a little bit about love that day. Finally the boy in me wasn't crying out for a kind of love my dad, young or old, could not give, and the man in me was content with loving him the way he wanted and needed to be loved. The love he was actually able to give was time in the garden, time in his world, not to mention the great tomatoes and squash. That day, the amount and kind of affection he was capable of giving was finally enough.

As Paul Harvey would say, "Now for the rest of the story." About a week later my father called. I nearly dropped the phone.

"Do you watch this show on television, *Who Wants to Be a Millionaire*?"

"Yeah, I've seen it a time or two."

"Well, you ought to watch it. There was this guy on the other night and he didn't win much money, but when Regis asked him what he did for a living he said he was an author of a book and then he said the title. Son, the next day thousands of people bought his book just because he said it on TV. John, you're the smartest man I know. You ought to try and get on the show and say your book's title, and maybe you'd win a lot of money and sell a lot of books at the same time."

I was forty-six years old, and to my recollection that was both the first time my father had ever called me—and the first time he had ever complimented my intelligence. I was floored;

it was almost an out-of-body experience. We talked about the show a little more and then hung up. I knew with everything in my bones that his phoning to give me an idea about book selling was the result of my going out to see his garden. I had given him what he longed for—respect and love for the man he is, a good man, a great gardener, a fair mechanic, machinist, and handyman. A man who like me had made hundreds of mistakes raising children, arranging his finances, and being a husband. The kind of mistakes we all make.

I gave him the kind of love he wanted, and he gave me the kind of love I had longed for. We connected. We have since been talking, emailing, saying *I love you,* spending time together, and getting to know each other as two aging, once ignorant men.

~

Dr. Patricia Allen in her book *Getting to "I Do"* talks about the need to be "Cherished and Adored" versus "Respected." These are slippery terms for a couple of reasons. First, they mean different things to different people. My first wife wanted to be the first to read my manuscript and to have her intellect respected; I wanted a roomful of flowers and gifts and the experience of having someone adore me.

My dad wanted to be cherished and adored. To him this would be achieved by me taking time for and showing interest in what he loved most—gardening, fixing things, building things. I on the other hand wanted him to respect my intelligence. I remembered his belittling me when I was a kid because I wasn't mechanical or sports-minded. I kept trying to get him to validate my intelligence by putting his intelligence down.

You may well ask, "Can't you be both cherished and respected?" Absolutely. If you are getting your primary need met—it might be respect at this stage of life—you will also feel cherished and adored. However, if only your secondary need is fulfilled, you won't really feel either. When my dear ex was respected, she also felt cherished and adored. When she cherished and adored me, I simultaneously felt loads of respect.

So what happens if you send people the kind of love they want and they still won't show you love the way you want to be loved? Unless they are active addicts, alcoholics, or suffering from extreme neurosis or psychosis, nine people out of ten almost always send you back the kind of love you need. If they don't, the fact that you broke out of your passivity and became a mature, active lover yourself will feel so good, it won't matter much.

The larger, more conscious question is: How do you know what kind of love your partner or family member longs for? The simple answer I always give is, "Ask." You would be surprised how unexpected this is to many people. Make sure you really listen, and even write down what others say so you won't forget.

How to Know Which Form of Love
You Need the Most Now

Draw a line down the center of a piece of paper. On the left side write Respect; *on the right,* Cherish and Adore. *On the left side, jot down everything you know about respect— what it would look like, feel like, sound like, and be like. Then do the same for cherish and adore on the right.*

The one you can say the least about is probably the one you have received very little of lately, or perhaps ever. The one you can say the most about is probably the one you need less at this point in your life.

Note: *You know the old saying,* Opposites attract? *Most (not all) people in relationships will experience this truth when it comes to the cherish-versus-respect conflict. Many are also wrong about their partner's primary need. I have worked with couples who've been together for decades, and when I ask them to write down which one they think their partner needs the most right now . . . they miss it. Don't assume. Ask.*

If you feel you still need more help with becoming a more active loving person, take a look at Gary Chapman's book *The Five Love Languages: How to Express Heartfelt Commitment to Your Mate.* Chapman believes everyone has a love tank, and that tank is filled by what he calls the five primary "love languages": Gifts, Words of Affirmation, Quality Time, Acts of Service, and Physical Touch. We want them all, but some are more important to us than others.

Chapman shows that we tend to give love in the languages we are most fluent in. This may be why a husband who does yard work, dishes, or car maintenance—Acts of Service—is totally surprised to hear his wife say, "You never show me you love me." But if he pressed further, she might reveal, "You never cuddle with me, or caress my hair, or give me long luxurious massages." In other words, she wants love in the language of Physical Touch. Or maybe she would complain, "You never want to spend time with me"—a plea for Quality Time. And some may hear, "Why don't you buy me flowers or write love poems like you used to do when we first got married," wanting Gifts. Or "You never tell me how much you appreciate me and what I do around the house"—seeking Words of Affirmation.

> *We tend to give love in the languages we are most fluent in.*

FURTHER THOUGHTS ON ACTIVE LOVING: THE FOUR FORMS OF LOVE

The English language is woefully lacking when it comes to words for expressing love. You know the silly ways we use the word—*I love my dog, I love my truck* (as a Southerner, I really do), *and I love my wife*. In the Greek language there are three words for love: *agape, philia,* and *eros*. In Latin there is a lovely word for love—*caritas*. In order to actively love, you can learn how to express all four.

The Greek word *agape* refers to spiritual love. *Philia* means a love for friends. *Eros* is a passionate love that might imply sexual yearnings (or might not), and the Latin *caritas* means love of community.

Getting to Nirvana

The Buddha spoke of Nirvana, the state of being where the selfishness that has most of us by the throat could be extinguished like a candle's flame. The way to reach this was by meditating on the Four Elements of Immeasurable Love that every one of us has access to:

Maitri: Loving kindness and the desire to help others achieve a deep level of happiness.

Karuna: Compassion for all those in pain and a desire to alleviate that pain and not cause more of it.

Mudita: A rigorous form of sympathetic joy that we experience when others are experiencing happiness.

Upeksha: An even mind and a commitment to love everyone equally and impartially.

You may be more fluent in one or two of these types of love rather than all four. In my first marriage there was plenty of *eros* but very little of the other three. In other words, we were not very loving friends, we did not involve the community in our relationship, and spiritual love was lacking as well. By the time I met and married my second wife, I knew that to actively love her I needed to increase my ability to love in all four ways. Although it didn't happen overnight, I involved friends and community in our relationship while experiencing plenty of *eros*. We are still working on applying *agape* by sharing our spiritual lives with each other in significant ways.

The more you and I integrate these four different love states into our relationships, the more exciting, stimulating, and invigorating we will be. This is a wonderful way to come out of residual passivity that loving only one or two ways keeps in place. As an exercise, look at the four kinds of love, writing down which ones you feel you are currently expressing in a significant, recognizable way and with whom. Which ones are expressed less often? How can you change that?

Passive Parenting/Passive Loving

Several months ago I was consulting with Tony, a precocious thirteen-year-old boy who eats, sleeps, and dreams of playing rock-and-roll guitar in a band. He practices every chance he gets. His father set up the appointment because he said Tony was getting into more and more trouble lately; he had tried everything he knew to discipline the boy, but nothing was working. After a few minutes I asked Tony, "So what's up with you and your dad?"

Without a moment's hesitation he replied, "I hate him. I can't stand him." I thought, *Well, nothing unusual here.* But when I asked him why, Tony took a deep breath and said, "Because he is so lame. He keeps pushing sports down my throat and I don't like sports; never have, never will, and he keeps saying that one day I will be grateful that he made me play. I hate him. He is so uncool."

"What did you tell him?"

"I've told him, 'Dude. I just want to play guitar and become a professional musician.' He laughs at me and says everyone wants to be a musician but almost no one can, and that sports will teach me discipline and teamwork and other bullshit. He keeps telling me that he didn't get to play sports when he was a kid because his father made him work in his sock factory so he could learn discipline and leadership, and he wants me to have what he never had. He just doesn't get me."

Tony's father was living his childhood dream vicariously through his son, a perfect example of passive parenting. By not loving Tony the way Tony desperately wanted and needed to be loved, his father was also engaging in passive loving.

The result was that Tony didn't feel truly seen and heard by his father—something Tony's father may have felt with his own dad. The passivity continues from generation to generation.

Authentic Contact

The first step in achieving real and meaningful connection with yourself as well as with another is to identify tired, worn-out patterns of behavior, speech, and thinking. These old patterns were usually created somewhere early in life as coping mechanisms to reduce conflict, pain, trauma, disappointment, or fear—and they worked for a while. But these same patterns can become fixed in your body like barnacles on the underbelly of boats. You can't see them unless you submerge into yourself and take a close look. Like barnacles, they only serve to weigh you down, not move you forward. These patterns then become repetitive reactions to people, places, and situations rather than the spontaneous responses that will rescue us from prolonged and pronounced passivity. Remember, passive and regressed people *react* while active, mature people *respond* to issues, conflicts, problems, and pain.

For genuine contact to prevail, these patterns must first be identified. Then the real work begins: We start going against the patterns to create new, untried ways of being, talking, and thinking. Here is the problem, though: Passive patterns produce a false sense of security and control. Breaking or

Remember, passive and regressed people react while active, mature people respond to issues, conflicts, problems, and pain.

going against the familiar is often messy, awkward, and even fear-producing because no one knows what will happen next.

Passive, pattern-sustaining people are like counterpunchers. In other words, when you say "A," I counterpunch with "B." I always have and always will, so we both know exactly how this encounter will end. Likewise when you do or say "C," I react with "D." Everybody knows where this will end, because we've done it a thousand times.

Ted, a very intelligent architect, expressed during a phone session, "I want to confront my father with some truths about his behaviors that really upset my wife when we go to visit. But I know what he will say, so why bother? It would just be a waste of my breath."

"Have you ever spoken to him about the issue that is distressing you and your wife?" I asked.

"I've tried confronting him before about other things, but we never get anywhere. He starts defending his behaviors, and I get pissed off and usually end up walking out of the house and swearing I won't go back."

"What would happen if you went against the patterns you just described? The next time you are with him, tell him how you feel, ask him not to interrupt, and don't walk out the door yourself no matter what he says or does."

"I don't know. I've never really tried that before. I'm sure he will cut me off and start defending. I know my dad."

"Have you ever once asked him before speaking to him not to interrupt? And have you ever once stayed and not left angry?"

"No. I guess I haven't."

What I went on to explain to Ted was what I've told hundreds of others: Patterns leave us stale and bored, and they perpetuate passivity. Breaking or going against patterns creates sparks of energy and enthusiasm—antidotes to poisonous passivity, pulling us out of sterility. It is identifying and breaking patterns that makes us search out fresh forms of human contact with those we care about, love, or work with. Most important, they help us stop taking what I call compensating actions and start taking inspired actions.

Breaking or going against patterns creates sparks of energy and enthusiasm.

COMPENSATING ACTIONS VERSUS INSPIRED ACTIONS

The patterns we have developed and perfected over the years were born of our efforts to compensate for our imagined or real weaknesses, failures, and defeats; our need to please or be perfect. Joseph, who was terribly awkward as a teenager, became the class clown not so much because he was naturally humorous but because every time he tried out for some sporting activity, his lack of athletic prowess embarrassed not only him, but his sports fanatic father. Joseph turned to comedy and even made his discontented father laugh at his antics and jokes. "I kept this up long after I really wanted to. I mean, for a while it got me girlfriends and got my dad off my back about my failure to be an all-star anything. But then it followed me into college and into my work life and I was 'sick unto death' to quote Kierkegaard or Camus, I can't remember which. When I wanted to talk about something deep, something that I was interested in, everyone kept expecting me to set up some kind of lame joke."

Cheryl understood. "I got so tired of playing the dumb blonde I could just throw up, but when I was a teenager the only way to really be popular was to hide how smart I really was and stick out my chest, pout my lips, and marvel at some boy's lesser intelligence." Cheryl, still stunning at sixty-two, went on, "I don't think I stopped playing that silly role until I was well into my forties."

Probably everyone reading this has found ways to compensate for certain issues chasing them into midlife. If these compensatory behaviors, attitudes, and actions are not serving us in the present, then we need to weed them out as quickly as possible in the second half of our lives.

Compensating actions are draining, exhausting, and ultimately please no one, including ourselves. When Willy's mistress demanded that he leave his wife, he ended the affair.

He then took his wife on a Caribbean cruise. However, his behavior was so disingenuous and false, all he and wife did the entire time was argue. "I felt drained of all energy and had absolutely no libido but I thought I was doing such a good thing trying to make up for my terrible behavior. She didn't seem to appreciate it at all."

Inspired Actions

To begin dismantling passivity and engage in inspired, genuine, and authentic ways of being—especially with those we really love and care about—it is important to really get clear how much of what we say and do, and don't say and don't do, is grounded in compensating behaviors. This is essential to identifying and breaking old patterns. Randal is in his mid-sixties. He is bright, energetic, and very passionate about seeing racism come to an end in his lifetime. He has worked tirelessly as an elementary history teacher and is a practitioner of Marshall Rosenberg's nonviolent communication teachings. For years he would try to get his father, who was born, raised, and steeped in prejudice and bigotry, to stop using the N-word when referring to African Americans. His pattern would be to try to teach his father about the history of civil rights in this country. "Dad, do you know who Rosa Parks was and what she did? Well, let me tell you." His father, a self-made millionaire who owned a contracting business, quit school in the ninth grade. Randal's lessons would turn his father back into a pimple-faced adolescent as he scolded him for not being more conscious.

When Randal clearly saw just how he engaged in patterns and compensatory behaviors in his interactions with his father, he was ready to employ a more inspired action the next time they got into a discussion.

"A year or so ago my dad was visiting and was talking about something he'd seen on television about Obama, and sure enough he pulled out the N-word. For the first time ever in my life I opened my mouth and spontaneously out popped the words, 'Stop, Dad, I don't want to hear that word spoken in this house.' It felt so honest and so real. He looked at me like I was a stranger, and I guess in a way I was. I had never done that before. He went on to say, 'Now, Randal, you know I don't mean anything by that word, it's just the way I was raised.'"

Randal continued, "A few months later he came to visit again. This time he was telling a story about how he'd run out of gas. He said, 'The damnedest thing happened, these two colored gentlemen picked me up and took me to get gas and brought me back and waited to make sure my car started. They were as fine a fellas as you'd ever want to meet.' I came out of my old teacher pattern and he came out of his old patterns. While he wasn't PC, it was a damn fresh start and improvement for me and my eighty-five-year-old dad."

ACTIVE THINKING

Emotions and feelings happen prior to thoughts. First come feelings; then come thoughts about the feelings. If you're feeling bad about yourself or others, then the thoughts that follow will be negative and passive, not positive and active. This is one major reason we have examined emotions and feelings so much in this book.

When the often painful developments of childhood and then puberty come to a screeching halt, our new growth pains must come from somewhere other than our ever-changing bodies. We must increase our engagement with people, projects, places, and things if we are to live fuller lives. Active thinking is just one of many ways to keep us from getting stale and bored and from boring others, especially those we live with and love.

If you're feeling bad about yourself or others, then the thoughts that follow will be negative and passive.

Passive people's minds are on strike. Their thinking tends to be rigid, overly consistent, and repetitive, versus the desired vibrant and imaginative outlook. They essentially see things the way they did twenty or forty years ago. Turning inward is usually the most emotionally and intellectually satisfying way to end our intellectual paralysis.

Going Inside

First we need to be clear that many passively inclined people think they go inward all the time—and many do spend inordinate amounts of time in morbid reflection and brooding. They revel in the past, get lost in reliving it, and ponder what has happened before, but nothing changes; no new behavior results from these constant trips down memory lane, which is only an emotional and mental cul-de-sac.

After being externally driven for so long—focused on work, raising kids, paying off mortgages, and any number of responsible behaviors—the second half of life offers time to add introspection to retrospection in exploring new inward territory.

Along with Robert Bly and others, I have been privileged to be considered an early pioneer of the "men's movement," a very misunderstood cultural phenomenon. While I won't go into detail here about its history, I will tell you that most of the men who participated and most of the women who encouraged it were squarely in the second half of their lives.

Unlike the women's and the civil rights movements, which were more externally directed and concerned with political and social change, the men's movement focused on going inward and changing the internal geography of men's hearts, souls, and minds. The emphasis was placed on men connecting at long last with buried, hidden, frozen, and lost feelings and emotions through poetry, myths, psychology, and experiential exercises. Sadly the novelty of the men's expressive movement, as it became known, made it the target of ridicule by some mainstream media, the negative attention chasing away the very men it sought to help: those dying early of heart attacks and finding themselves alienated from wives, lovers, and children.

Luckily it did have a lasting effect on the millions of men and women who were ready to make the internal journey and whose emotional and intellectual intelligences were enhanced. It continues to serve as another tool to relieve paralyzing passivity and shake off emotional numbness.

ENHANCING EMOTIONAL INTELLIGENCE

One of the most active ways to come out of passivity is to increase and elevate your emotional intelligence quotient (EQ). Enhancing your EQ makes you a more emotionally available partner, parent, or spouse and allows you to be more intimate and feel more connected to those you care about. At the same time, you'll be better equipped to succeed as a boss, employee, colleague, and friend.

During the last decade emotional intelligence has become a key factor in achieving success in everything from romantic

Each day we make literally hundreds of decisions that require us to be in tune with our emotional selves.

relationships to a corporation's bottom line. Each day we make literally hundreds of decisions that require us to be in tune with our emotional selves; decisions that can't be made with reason and rational thought alone. Author Daniel Goleman describes it well: "Emotional Intelligence refers to the ability to sense, understand, value, and effectively apply the power and acumen of emotions as a source of human energy, information, trust, creativity, and influence."

Interestingly, studies show that a person's IQ (intelligence quotient) is set by age twenty or twenty-one, but emotional intelligence can be increased anytime at any stage in a person's life.

EQ is rapidly becoming more important when it comes to hiring a manager or picking a mate because, as many of us have experienced, a high IQ does not equal activity, happiness, or success, but a high EQ does. Whereas a person's IQ was once the standard used to hire corporate executives or other high-powered positions, that is now becoming secondary to a person's EQ.

SETTING BOUNDARIES

There are many ways to increase your emotional intelligence. One very important activity that is seldom discussed is the process of building and maintaining boundaries. Strong boundaries can replace the walls erected by passivity.

Boundaries are lines that you draw in the sand, on the carpet, in the air, in your soul, in your body, and in life in general. These are lines that others can't cross without consequences and repercussions. These boundaries are not imaginary, though you may not be able to see them. They say, *This is how close you can come to me—physically, emotionally, spiritually, financially, sexually, and verbally.*

Passive people build walls to hide behind, avoiding conflict and confrontation and generally withdrawing from the world to greater or lesser degrees. But they do not allow you to be your authentic self. You can tell the difference between a healthy boundary and a wall of passivity by looking at your family and friends to see if they *Strong boundaries can replace the walls erected by passivity.* have flat heads from banging them against your walls or calluses on their hands from trying to tear them down. Many of us know more about wall construction than boundary building.

Boundaries, if created and defended appropriately, will not only make you feel safe, but also help keep you from feeling overwhelmed, which is one of many fears a passive person deals with almost daily. With good boundaries, the walls of passivity that cut off your own and other people's emotions are no longer necessary. Boundaries are what will keep you and others safe to feel whatever you need to feel at the moment. This is because you will not feel violated, offended, abused, or exhausted nearly as often. Boundaries will enhance communication, clarity, and emotional connection to those you care about or work with.

Boundaries help us to separate our thoughts and feelings from those of other people—including but not limited to our parents, children, spouses, and friends. Collapsing, merging, or enmeshing with others is a major problem for passively inclined people. Boundaries help show us where we begin and end—and where someone else begins and ends—by establishing the appropriate psychological, emotional, and physical space between us.

Emotional boundaries can include how much or how little of someone's anger, sadness, fear, or joy you will allow to come toward you before you have had enough or become overwhelmed. These emotional boundaries say to yourself and others: *Your anger or fear is yours, not mine,* and vice versa.

Emotional boundaries say to yourself and others: Your anger or fear is yours, not mine, *and vice versa.*

For example, sexual boundaries can communicate that it is all right for someone to hold your hand, but that's all. The other person can put an arm around you but go no farther. No one can touch your children sexually. And so on.

Informational boundaries announce when you have had enough about this or that subject or person. You don't want to hear or take in any more because you may get overstimulated.

Financial boundaries acknowledge that you will talk to your boss about how much he pays you, but not your neighbor. You may talk to your father about what you paid for your home, but not your doctor. Your accountant and banker will have greater access to your financial life, but you don't share that information with acquaintances or social friends.

Spiritual boundaries monitor what comes into your spiritual being. They allow you to choose who can give you spiritual advice, solace, or comfort. Perhaps your minister, priest, rabbi, or imam—but not the person pounding on the door or crying on the television.

Good, clear boundaries are also highly effective in dealing with and negotiating stress, anxiety, conflicts, confrontation, and intimacy. Boundaries can reduce tension, friction, and misunderstanding. They also, believe it or not, can increase connection and comfort. If *you* know where you begin and end and *I* know where I begin and end, we don't have to worry about encroachment, abandonment, invasion, or oppression.

A word of caution: As with any new insight or information, the first time you use your boundaries with unhealthy people, they will often react negatively. They may get angry or even enraged with you and try to talk you out of your new psychological and emotional equipment for managing your life better. "You are just putting walls up between us," "Why aren't you allowing me access to these parts of your life like you used to?"

Initially you may doubt your ability to create healthy boundaries. "You're becoming rigid," and so on. You may even question yourself: "Am I being too inflexible?" "Are these really walls?" Initially you may doubt your ability to create healthy boundaries. And don't be surprised if in the beginning your boundaries may be a little over the top—you may at first go from no boundaries to all boundaries. This can be adjusted as time goes on.

A Boundary That Isn't Defended Isn't a Boundary

An important part of coming out of passivity and setting good boundaries is to stick with them *and* appropriately defend them, when necessary. A boundary that can't be defended isn't a real boundary but just a really good idea. At a Boundaries and Limits workshop, one participant shared his story. "I set good boundaries with my mother when I go to see her but she refuses to acknowledge them. But it's not because I don't have them, she just ignores them," Theo said.

"Then they're not really boundaries because real boundaries can't be ignored. Think of the fence around your house. If you don't open the gate, or tear down the fence, or let your neighbor tear it down, then they can't come into your space. Do you agree?" I asked him.

"No, I don't. See, I go over for dinner every Sunday. She's all alone now that my father is dead. I put on my plate what I want to eat and then she puts food on my plate that *she* wants me to eat, such as brussels sprouts, which I hate. I tell her I don't want them and I don't want her to put food on my plate, that it's my plate!" He paused, obviously upset.

"So what happened?" one of the workshop participants asked.

Theo continued his story. "She puts the food on every time. I set a boundary and she ignores it every time. It's not that I don't make boundaries clear."

I asked this man, who owned his own auto repair shop, how old he was.

"I'll be thirty-two next month. What has that got to do with anything? What do you want me to do?" he said, his face getting red with anger. "Throw the food in her face? She's my mother, for Christ's sake."

"No, that would be rage, not defending a boundary."

Another workshop participant offered this suggestion. "How about saying something like, 'Mom, if you keep putting food on my plate, I'm leaving'?"

From all the nodding in the room, I could tell most of the workshop participants liked that idea, but it wasn't the right choice, either. "No, that's a threat," I said.

Most of the people I've worked with who have boundary issues tend to think there are really only two ways to defend a boundary. One is to leave the person (a very passive reaction) who tends to ignore their boundaries; the other is to perform a violent or aggressive act, much like Theo's "Throw the food in her face."

So what would be a good way for Theo to defend his boundaries with his mother? Next time he speaks to her, he could say, "Mom, I won't be coming home for Sunday dinner anymore. I'll be coming over on Sunday afternoon for tea only." Or, "Mom, I've already eaten, I'll sit here and watch you eat." If she asks him why not, he can answer, "When I'm eating with you, I don't feel respected."

There are options other than just fight or flight, but Theo's vision was clouded and obviously his issue with his mother was of long standing.

Saying *NO*—A Great Boundary Word

If you don't want to use walls to shield yourself from your own and other people's emotions, what do you do? You learn to say and mean the following words and statements, which many passive people almost never say and mean:

- No!
- No more!
- Enough!
- Stop!
- This doesn't work for me!

"No" is a complete sentence. As the famous (or infamous) Gestalt therapist Fritz Perls said, "If you can't say 'No,' then your 'Yes' doesn't mean a damn thing." Passive people are constantly playing the role of the yes-man or -woman to the detriment of their own physical, emotional, and spiritual well-being. Why is it so difficult to say, "Stop, I don't want to hear any more. No more! Enough!"? Because in trying to do so, many of us regress to a time, usually childhood, when these words were not allowed or our primary role models could not use them successfully without negative consequences.

"No" is a complete sentence.

There are other active ways to stop and defend boundary violations, encroachments, and invasions:

- **Identify the specific violation:** "When you don't knock before coming into my room . . ."

- **Tell the person how you feel** when your space, needs, and feelings are not respected: "I get angry and scared . . ."

- **Add energy, body language, and sterner words:** Say "I'm serious about this" while putting up your hand in a stop motion or planting your feet firmly.

Know what you will do and won't do should the violation continue or occur again (*I will look for another place to live and move out*). It is important that you know your plan, but it is also very important that you don't tell other adults.

If you convey the consequences to other adults verbally, they will more often than not interpret your words as a threat or ultimatum. However, do tell children what the consequences will be should they violate or disregard your boundaries, so they can learn to make healthy choices in the future.

FINDING YOUR LIMITS

For passive people, limits are even more of a mystery than boundaries. Even professional therapists can confuse the two.

A boundary says, "This is how close you can come to me." A limit says, "This is how far I'll go."

In a nutshell a *boundary* says, "This is how close you can come to me." A *limit* says, "This is how far I'll go." It is the emotional and intellectual knowledge of how you'll respond in a particular situation.

Many people have trouble knowing what their limits are in both personal and professional circumstances. Mary, a compassionate and thoughtful mother and owner of a resale clothing store, is an example. "I'm so angry with my son I don't know what to do" were her first words to me after hello. "I told him I would put him through two alcohol and drug treatment programs and then he's on his own."

"How is that going?" I asked.

"Not too well. That's why I'm so mad at him. I have now put him through four of the best and most expensive treatment centers in the country."

"Mary," I said, "what are your limits?"

She fired back, "I said two. But obviously it wasn't. That's why I'm so angry."

"So you don't know your limits and you're angry with him because he doesn't know them, either?"

Mary laughed and said, "Oh!"

Setting limits can actually lead to deeper connections with those we care about. When we don't know our limits, we go much farther, or stop very short of where we want to be in regard to how much we want to do with or for someone.

Not knowing what our limits are can turn us into passive caretakers instead of active caregivers. Care*givers* have good boundaries and know their limits. Care*takers* go way beyond and farther than they really want to go. Caretakers actually end up taking something out of those they are around—like their integrity, energy, self-esteem, or the money they find underneath the cushions on the couch. Those who don't know or pay attention to their limits tend to feel resentment and therefore need some kind of payment or restitution, to actually take something for giving up something of themselves that they really do not want to give. Adults who know and respect their own limits can care for others without resentment, without feeling like something is being taken from them. They actually feel energized by their giving to others. This is what I call being compassionately assertive—more about that later.

*Caregivers have good boundaries and know their limits. Care*takers *go way beyond and farther than they really want to go.* When we listen to our own internal rhythms for closeness and separateness, we know what our limits are. If we stay true to our rhythms, we know how long we can visit our parents without falling into old, destructive conversations and patterns. If we know when to seek solitude to recharge our batteries, then we won't have to push people away or run away from a relationship just because we can't say, "I need some time alone."

Another client of mine was having trouble interacting with his father. I asked Terry how long he thought he could be with him before feeling overwhelmed. "Maybe thirty minutes. Then I'll become his little boy again and we'll be in the same old dysfunctional drama we're always in."

"What about just staying thirty minutes or less, if that's your limit?" I asked.

"We'd probably enjoy each other's company. I'd leave on a good note because I'd still be an adult instead of a pissed-off kid who didn't want to ever come back."

Limits not only help us establish the difference between caregiving and caretaking, they separate quantity from quality. Terry recognized that if he respected his own limits and kept to thirty-minute visits, when his father died it would be after a compassionate exchange of time, energy, respect, and love, not a resentful one.

Here are a few more examples of less dramatic ways to think about limits:

- I'll only be able to go one more week.

- I'll explain this two more times.

- I can talk about this for thirty minutes.

- I'll give my boss one month to respond to my request.

Let's recap. As emotionally intelligent, active adults, we can easily set boundaries and limits that can be pulled in, extended, or shifted based on choice, new information, or more experience, depending on the individual situations and people. Our boundaries and limits are clear to us and to those we live with, love, or work with. Good boundaries and limits help protect us without isolating or pushing people away. They keep us at a safe distance so that we don't have to accept anyone's rage, shaming, or abusive words, actions, or demeaning behaviors.

Good boundaries and limits help protect us without isolating or pushing people away.

Good boundaries and limits actually increase intimacy, clarity, communication, and vulnerability because they allow us to say no when we need to. You can also say yes when you want to. You know where you stand, and this allows others to know more about you. It enhances their feelings of safety and trust because they can rely on you when you say: "No more," "Enough," "Stop," or, "It's okay, you can come closer." When we don't compromise our boundaries and limits no matter what others may think but stay true to ourselves, everyone involved wins in the long run of any relationship.

PART 3

BECOMING COMPASSIONATELY ASSERTIVE IN THE SECOND HALF OF LIFE

There are dozens of books written about compassion, and more books written about assertiveness than I care to count. However, no one has put the two together. That is my task. Let's get started.

The word *compassion* is often confused with the word *pity,* a misuse furthered by the *Oxford Dictionary* defining *compassionate* as "piteous" or "pitiable." The word *compassion* literally means "with passion"—possessing a feeling of enthusiasm or a compelling emotion toward a person, place, object, or process.

Compassion—from the Latin word *patiri* and the Greek *pathein*—means "to undergo or experience or endure something with another person." It is close to empathy, but with more vigor.

Becoming compassionately assertive means to have enthusiasm coupled with emotion as well as a huge dose of vigorous empathy. This keeps us from being abusive, aggressive, hostile, or willing to say or do anything to win a discussion, argument, confrontation, or battle.

When we read about or personally know people who are truly passionate, we admire them. If we emulate them, our experiences in all areas of life are richer and more satisfying.

The labels *assertive* or *assertiveness* are very often confused with *aggressive* and *aggressiveness*. *Assertive* refers to behavior characterized by confidence. Assertive people are willing to clearly declare or affirm their position, feeling, emotion, or statement without needing to prove it to anyone's satisfaction. They achieve this without threatening another person's feelings or point of view, and therefore the listener does not need to feel defensive or submissive.

Assertive refers to behavior characterized by confidence.

Passive people are not assertive. They do not defend their own personal positions, attitudes, beliefs, or feelings. They allow aggressive people to abuse or manipulate them because of fear. Passive men and women typically do not try to influence anyone else or change their minds; they see that as the job of debaters and negotiators.

Compassionate assertiveness is the antidote to passivity. We communicate assertively by overcoming our fear of speaking our minds or trying to influence others. The trick is to do so in a way that respects the personal boundaries of others.

Assertive people are also willing to defend themselves against aggressive people.

Compassionate assertiveness is the antidote to passivity.

Where aggressive or passive people are forever judging, threatening, lying to themselves and others, breaking confidences, putting up walls, and violating others' boundaries, compassionately assertive people strive for cooperation via honest expression of feelings and personal truths.

One of the main keys to becoming more and more compassionately assertive during discussions, conflicts, and confrontations is to remain issue-focused rather than person-focused.

Samantha is a sixty-year-old book editor for a major publishing house. Her husband, Rubin, is a retired stockbroker. Samantha is disturbed by how many hours each day Rubin spends sitting in his La-Z-Boy recliner watching television.

"Years ago I would have said, 'How can you watch so many terrible shows all day long? I hate that you are watching so much TV.' Now I tell him that I think most television is dull and boring and it can become addictive."

In other words Samantha talked about television as an issue rather than belittling or demeaning her husband for the hours he passed watching it.

How much television her husband watches is really none of her business but how she feels about it *is,* and it is her job

Characteristics of the Compassionately Assertive

- *They feel free to express their feelings, thoughts, and desires.*
- *They are able to initiate and maintain comfortable relationships with other people.*
- *They know their rights.*
- *They have clear boundaries and limits and respect those of others at all times.*
- *They have control over their anger and share it appropriately in a nonthreatening way. This does not mean that they repress their anger; it means that they control it and talk about it in a reasoning manner.*
- *They are willing to compromise with others, rather than always wanting their own way.*
- *They tend to have good self-esteem.*
- *They are continually in the process of being less and less focused on other people's needs, wishes, wants, and thoughts.*
- *They enter and exit friendships and business arrangements without bitterness and resentment.*

to communicate these feelings in a compassionately assertive way. They end up telling her husband more about her and almost nothing about him.

How much your wife works is none of your business; how you feel about it is. But discussing your feelings as they impact the marriage is important and much more constructive than accusations of a character defect or flaw in the person doing the working.

As I have said earlier, most of what we think is our business is not—we would all be happier if we'd live and let live, keeping our side of the street clean and not monitoring or criticizing how poorly someone is tending to theirs. Passive and aggressive people think everybody's business is their business, and their role here on Earth is to point out what everyone else is doing wrong. There is no compassion in this position.

BECOMING COMPASSIONATELY ASSERTIVE

You have tried to be nice and sensitive—that didn't work. You have tried to stuff your feelings and emotions and bottle them up, gunny-sack them, store them in your warehouse of a body and brain—that didn't work, either. You tried to be aggressive and blow people out of the water with your Howitzer words and the excessive energy of a nuclear-powered turbine. Guess what? That didn't work for anyone. Now you're ready to try becoming compassionately assertive with those you love, care about, or work with. Sounds good, doesn't it? But how do you do it?

The good news is that if you've gotten this far in the book, you have laid the important groundwork. Now all you have to do is pull it all together and practice, practice, practice until you're ready to give your recital at the Carnegie Hall of Mental and Emotional Health.

First let's look at the word *becoming*. It is a process. You are not going to achieve perfection. After decades of trying the other futile options, it will take a while to get this new one.

Passion is what the word *compassionate* is built on. If you are still clinging to residual passivity and not moving toward your own passions, then you are not being compassionate with yourself. This makes being compassionate with others almost unachievable.

Assertiveness without compassion, calmness, and maturity is just a proving ground for being aggressive or passive-aggressive. Keep in mind these four easy steps:

Step 1. Identify what upsets, angers, annoys, frustrates, or intimidates you, or makes you fearful.

Example: Bill says his wife threatens him several times each month with the possibility of divorce. He confesses, "I don't know what to say. The last time she told me, I said, 'I hear you feel neglected and unloved.' That didn't do anything."

"What would you have liked to have said if you weren't trying so hard to be sensitive and nice and you weren't afraid of her reaction?" I asked.

"I would like to have said, 'Goddamn it! Don't talk to me like this. I'm sick and tired of hearing this kind of crap.'" (Note: If you don't have a therapist, counselor, good friend, sponsor, or someone who can listen without judgment, simply write your words on a piece of paper to be thrown away or burned later.)

Step 2. Try to tell someone appropriately how you feel.

Example: "This really doesn't work for me anymore. I am very angry and upset hearing this over and over and really wish you would think about stopping using this threatening language. This doesn't work for me . . . This doesn't work for me."

Bill went on for another two or three minutes and he did pretty well with staying in the realm of expressing himself passionately and appropriately.

Step 3. Take what you wish you had said or done and break it down to a clear, concise, five- to seven-word statement.

Example: "Threatening doesn't work for me." Bill repeated this three times in step 2. This core phrase expresses his deep feeling in a very compassionately assertive manner. The result is no one is hurt, and no one is confused about Bill's feelings and message.

Step 4. Use any one of the four compassionately assertive words that almost no one ever uses when they are angry, hurt, frustrated, or fearful:

- Stop

- Enough

- No

- No more

Example: "Stop. Threatening doesn't work for me."

By not being afraid to say what he really means in a compassionately assertive manner, he will shorten the dialogue and likely end any misunderstanding.

Very often in our pseudo-niceness or attempts to be sensitive, we end up saying five hundred or sometimes five thousand words to keep from using the words above. When we finish our tirade, the listener may respond in confusion: "What are you trying to say exactly?" We pad our conversation with meaningless or harmful words in an attempt not to hurt the other person's feelings. But we end up doing just that.

> **Dropping the Passivity and Becoming Compassionately Assertive**
> - *Take risks in relationships.*
> - *Push through resistances.*
> - *Overcome fears of engulfment and abandonment.*
> - *Stop fixing others.*

- *Prioritize.*
- *Ask the right question—How well am I loving?*
- *Slow down.*
- *Increase independence.*
- *Build a support system.*
- *Avoid repetition compulsion.*
- *Think in a way that is problem-focused and inventive rather than routine.*
- *Use freshly coined, selectively chosen language, instead of slogans and clichés.*
- *Explore new territories.*
- *Apply a certain, safe measure of self-exposure.*
- *Develop and refine mental skills.*
- *Expand and increase your range of emotions.*
- *Use self-made resources rather than borrowed or vicarious resources.*
- *Develop a richer inner life.*
- *Engage in body-centered psychology.*
- *Stop exaggerating shortcomings; instead, validate your own strengths.*
- *Give up victim language. ("He keeps ignoring my boundaries.")*
- *Grieve the losses, changes, and transitions.*
- *Find the balance between your personal and your professional life.*
- *Do anger work on an ongoing basis.*

Getting Rid of the Word *You*

Sometimes the three-letter word *y-o-u* is so offensive that it ought to be a four-letter word. *You* acts as a trigger to many people, especially during a conflict or intense conversation. In the last decade or so, many therapists and counselors have passed on to their clients the tool we will call "When you _____, I feel _____." Although this is a huge step in communication, it still contains the word *you*. I have been showing clients and workshop participants an alternative expression that better suits becoming more compassionately assertive: *I* statements and looking a person in the eye.

Aggressive people tell you more about you than about themselves. They'll tell you what you should and should not do, feel, or say. When they finish trying to control you, they often think what they've communicated is "for your own good" or because they love and care about you.

Passive people let themselves be told about themselves for hours and years before the resentment finally sets in and they have enough.

Compassionately assertive people use the word *I* and tell you about themselves. By simply swapping the two, you can see how the word *you* is one of the most simultaneously passive and aggressive ways of speaking because it is usually rooted in unsolicited criticism or advice giving.

Examples:

"I need this to stop now" versus "You need to stop now."

"I can't continue the conversation at this time" versus "You
should stop talking now."

"I feel a need to rest now"
versus "You look tired. You
should rest now."

*Aggressive people
tell you more about
you than about
themselves.*

"I am feeling very angry right now" versus "You look very
angry right now."

"I am feeling overwhelmed by this conversation" versus
"You are overwhelming me right now."

You implies I know better than you. *You* says, *I am the
teacher and you are my student. "You* says, *I am the winner
and you are the loser. You* very often is shaming, demeaning,
demoralizing, judging, and analyzing. And by the way, so are
most of the things we do when we think we are telling someone how we feel—we shame, judge, demean, and so on.

Perhaps you recall the example I gave earlier when Randal said to his father, "I need to not hear the N-word spoken in my presence." That statement conveys to his father
who he is, what he feels, and what his deepest needs are.
It is a way for his father to know his son and his values. In
contrast, simply telling his father, "You need to stop using
the N-word" implies criticism that his father didn't ask for,

a judgment of him that neither he nor anyone in his family wanted.

Confrontations with compassionately assertive people usually end in a win–win scenario because they tend to be calm rather than co-dependent, raising their awareness of the other person's feelings while staying true to their own. They also know how to say no if necessary; they can stand up for themselves, assert their rights and feelings, create and defend boundaries, and set reasonable limits. Compassionately assertive men and women have no intent to hurt or damage and can refrain from overreacting.

The Right Kind of Criticism

The way most people give criticism is dysfunctional and ends up hurting others. The right way to give criticism is if you are asked to give it; the criticism is also purposeful and meant to help the person who asks for it.

For example, take this book you hold in your hands. I've asked my wife, who is a talented editor and writer, to read it and give her critical assessment and feedback. My editor has read and re-read it and offered more advice and good suggestions regarding what to leave in and what to leave out. After this book is in print, however, I won't be open to criticism unless I specifically ask for it.

Compassionately assertive people know they don't have to explain or justify their feelings, thoughts, or actions to anyone unless they want to.

Passive/Aggressive/Compassionately Assertive Conversations

Passive	Aggressive	Compassionately Assertive
If it's all right with you, I'd like to tell you how I really feel about _____.	*Sit down, we're going to talk about _____ whether you want to or not.*	*I need to say how I feel about _____.*
I'm wondering if you wouldn't mind doing the shopping today?	*You do the shopping today; after all, it's your turn. I did it last week.*	*I'm not able to go grocery shopping today.*
I know this might not work for you, but could we come to your house for dinner if it's not too much to ask?	*I'm coming over for dinner and if you have other plans, cancel them.*	*I would like to come to your house for dinner; I'm too tired to cook.*

Compassionately assertive people can decide when they're ready or willing to listen to someone else share feelings as well.

Because truly compassionately assertive people respect themselves, they extend that respect and civility to others. As Judith McClure says in her book *Civilized Assertiveness for Women*, "Civility is ethical behavior toward others. Assertiveness is ethical behavior toward ourselves." We can't show the former if we don't embody the latter.

THE FOUR COMPASSIONATELY ASSERTIVE STATEMENTS

There are four statements that, if considered, contemplated, and completed, will enhance clarity and communication and diminish misunderstanding. They will work for virtually every issue, conflict, decision, and interaction, whether personal or professional. They are:

1. This is what I want: _____.

2. This is what I need: _____.

3. This is what I will not do to get the above wants and needs met, achieved, or accomplished:

    _____.

4. This is what I will do to get these wants and needs met, achieved, or accomplished: _____.

The first statement is designed to let you say your best-case scenario. It tells listeners what your fantasy about any situation or problem is without criticizing or demeaning them.

The second statement is your "bottom line." This portion of the conversation is usually non-negotiable. It is almost like food, water, air, and love. You can't settle for less now that you are no longer passive. You are actively in charge of securing your needs.

The third statement is a clear message of what you will not do to get your wants and needs met. For instance, you will not bribe, coerce, threaten, et cetera.

The fourth and final statement is a clear, concise wording of what you are willing to do to get your wants and needs met at this time or in the very near future.

The following are examples of the four compassionately assertive statements as used by my clients and workshop participants over the years. If one or both parties employ this technique regularly, a level of intimacy and authenticity will be achieved in ways only dreamed about by many who in their passivity refuse to step up to the plate.

Cynthia's main problem in her marriage—as she identified it—was that her husband worked all the time. "He works as much as eighty hours a week. I know he wants a good life for me and the kids, but we hardly ever see him and when we do he's exhausted or asleep."

"What do you want?" I asked her to write it down. Wants are your best-case scenarios, your fantasy fulfilled, your magic wand waved and presto-changeo they happen, no questions asked.

"I want him to make more time for us and the kids, and I want him to work less," she said after taking a few moments.

"What do you need regarding this problem or issue?" This question is considerably different from the first, and usually more difficult to answer. Needs are not open for compromise the way wants may be. Needs are what you must have and can't live without.

Cynthia took about ten or fifteen minutes on this part. After she wrote, she looked up and said, "I need one evening every week for the two of us to talk, make love, or just cuddle and watch a movie. I need him to take better care of himself so he can be more present and available for our children." She paused. "That sounds so selfish. Am I being too self-centered to need this? Maybe I'm too demanding."

"Let's see," I said. "How you have gone about trying to get those needs and wants met in the past?"

"Well, that's easy," she replied, laughing. "I just nagged, complained, and criticized him for the last couple of years. I guess that's being more selfish than saying straight out what I need."

"Okay. Next, what will you not do to get these wants and needs met?"

"I won't nag or criticize him anymore. I won't try to be both mother and father to the kids to make up for his lack of interaction and attention. I won't speak badly about him anymore." Note that these things are about setting good boundaries, establishing limits, and not being co-dependent, passive, or a martyr.

"Okay, Cynthia," I said. "Now what will you do to get your wants and needs met?"

Again she took about ten or fifteen minutes before answering.

"I will speak my truth. I will set good boundaries and limits. I will support him in any way I can, even if that means my going back to work at least part-time. I will watch household expenses and my spending so he won't feel so pressured by money issues. I will love him no matter what. I will tell him so and also how much I appreciate all the things he does for this family." She took a deep breath and let out a heavy sigh. "Why weren't we taught to talk like this before?"

Then she asked a question that I frequently get: "When is the best time to do this exercise?" The absolute best time is when you and the other person are in a good place. When you're rested and refreshed and have not argued or fought recently about a particular issue. Sadly, most people try to tell other people their wants and needs in the middle or at the end of a major confrontation, when everyone is regressed, exhausted, or scared. This also means they are not heard—or, worse, their wants and needs are interpreted as more pressure, stress, ultimatums, or threats.

Many are loath to bring up conflict issues when things are going smoothly. It seems unfair. What is really unfair and more hurtful and damaging is passively holding in these things until they erupt and get blurted out with no regard for the rage that usually follows.

Here's another example using the four compassionate assertive statements.

Mark works at a building supply company for a boss who is less than appreciative of his efforts. "I've worked there for three and a half years and the man has never once complimented me or given me a raise. He has me managing the section of the store I know the least about. I keep asking to be transferred into the yard and garden section. I know plants and flowers better than anyone at the store. I stay frustrated and angry most of my working hours," he said, looking disgusted with the whole situation.

"Okay, got it. What do you want?"

"I want to be in the garden section. I want my boss to appreciate how hard I work and tell me every blue moon or so. I want a raise in pay and I want to enjoy where I work. Yeah, that's about it."

"What do you need?"

He answered as quickly as anyone I've worked with. "I need respect, appreciation, and to enjoy where I work. That's not asking too much, is it?"

"What will you not do to get your wants and needs met in this situation?"

On this one he took some time. Eventually he responded, "I will not work anywhere or for anyone that doesn't appreciate me. My boss needs to eventually place me where I can be the best at what I do."

"What will you do to get your wants and needs met?" He took even more time and wrote in his journal before answering. "I will ask my boss for a performance evaluation at least every six months. I will tell him I am not being used efficiently in the department I'm in and request a transfer into the garden department as soon as that is possible."

"How does it feel to say all of this with such clarity and consciousness?" I asked.

"Great! And you know, my boss is a pretty smart fellow or he wouldn't be in the position he is in, so I bet he'll listen to me. But if he doesn't respond within three to six months at the most, then I'll look for a place where my strengths can be put to good use."

With that, Mark set his limits with his boss.

You can see in both examples that Cynthia and Mark are trying to be compassionately assertive. If their respective counterparts can hear them—and they probably will—there will be much more satisfying outcomes than if they continued to rage, regress, shame, blame, criticize, or judge. They are being compassionate toward themselves first, and then extending that compassion to the others in their lives. Cynthia's children will benefit. Mark's family will benefit, too. Being compassionately assertive comes with incalculable fringe benefits.

DETACHING VERSUS DISCONNECTING

An expectation is a yet-to-be-realized resentment. Just because you come out of your passivity and learn to become compassionately assertive does not mean you will always be received with grace and respect. It does, however, increase that likelihood dramatically. So in order to become more compassionate people, we have to detach ourselves from the outcome. The goal is to detach from our preconceptions of how people are to behave, react, or respond to us, especially during confrontations and conflicts.

Detachment is not the cold, calculated emotional stance that some people think it is. What is really cold is slipping back into passivity and using a negative response as something to put between us and those we care about. If we act in a compassionately asser-tive manner but are met with a negative response, we may be tempted to disconnect, sometimes for days, months, and even years. The walls of silence still get thicker and thicker with every phone call not taken, every e-mail not responded to, and every visit that is postponed or canceled altogether.

An expectation is a yet-to-be-realized resentment.

Detachment is simply remembering this: *Most of what I think is my business is none of my business, and that includes how someone feels or thinks about me after I have been authentic and compassionately assertive with them.* It allows us to say to them, *I care about you and what you are going through, but I also trust that you can handle your life, business, finances, children, parents, or problems. I will be there for you should you ask for my help, support, advice, or counsel.*

Detachment is also based on empathy rather than sympathy. *Sympathy* and *empathy* are two words that often get used interchangeably, as if they mean the same thing. They don't.

Sympathy says *I will feel what you feel. If you are sad, angry, hurt, or afraid then I am, too.* Empathy means *I understand some of what you are going through because I have been through similar experiences myself.* Sympathy tends to convey *I am capable of dealing with your issues even though you are not,* which makes me superior and you inferior. Sympathy tends to be draining and exhausting over the long haul of any relationship. In contrast, empathy elevates the person we are supporting and actually energizes everyone involved. You may not have experienced what someone has been through exactly, but you have experienced something close. For example, you may not have ever had a spouse die, but you have experienced the loss of a loved one. You can show empathy for someone else's loss even if your own wasn't exactly the same.

> *Sympathy tends to be draining and exhausting over the long haul of any relationship.*

Troy's mother and father's marriage had been Troy's business ever since he was a child—or so he thought and felt until he attended the Half-Lived Life workshop. He had a good basis for this: His mother had been telling him about his father's failings since she shared news of his adultery when Troy was only five years old. Troy, who later became a social worker, had given his parents books on marriage and paid to send them to a marriage seminar with one of the leaders in the field.

I told Troy that how he felt about his parents' marriage was his business but the marriage itself was not. In other words, he could feel however he wanted about his parents' marriage—angry, upset, and disappointed—but he had no right to interfere, complain, or criticize them when they were present. He looked at me, stunned. "But they are my parents and what if I can help them? Am I to say nothing?"

"How has saying anything worked so far?" I gently asked.

"Not so well. They get angry with me and I get really mad at them. I'm just trying to help, for God's sake."

Troy went on to tell the group that over the last couple of years he has gone home to visit less and less and was thinking about not going at all for Christmas holidays, "Because all they will do is argue and fight."

While detaching is active and compassionate, distancing or disconnecting is more often than not inappropriate and regressive behavior.

REGRESSION AND REGRESSIVE BEHAVIORS

Passivity is a form that regression can take. There are many ways to define emotional regression—feeling small or little, feeling less than the age we really are, an unconscious return to a previous time in our history, or just plain losing it. You're probably very familiar with the following examples of how we express ourselves when we see someone we think is regressing—either you've employed them recently or someone has said them to you:

"I wish you'd grow up."

"You're pouting like a big baby."

Perhaps a less common—but still a good—way to define *regression* is as an unconscious return to our past history. The more passive people are, the more they tend to relive their past patterns. When we regress, we are hurled into our past faster than lightning. We say or react the way we did when we were in our twenties, teens, or late or early childhood. This is not the same as consciously drawing on the past to solve a current problem by thinking back and remembering how we solved a similar issue in the past. Rather, it is an unconscious and unintentional revisiting of deep feelings and reactions we felt at one time and find ourselves reliving over and over.

The best example of this is occurs for many people when they go home for the holidays. Approaching our parents' driveways, we're still feeling like adults. Once we cross the threshold, Mom and Dad start talking or interacting with us like they did thirty years ago. Before you know it, we're talking to them just like we did when we were twelve or thirteen—sometimes even repeating ourselves word for word.

Sharon knows that it isn't long before the regressive behavior begins when she goes home for a visit. Her mother, who is in her mid-seventies, starts commenting about her clothes or hair. Sharon says, "My mom gives me a warm hug then steps back, gently brushes my hair away, and says the same thing: 'Honey, why don't you get your hair out of your face. You have such a pretty face. People want to see your beautiful face.' I want to ignore her but instead I say, 'Mom, it's my hair and my face and I'll wear it any way I want to.' I'm forty-four years old, for God's sake. When does it stop?"

Bob shares, "Every time I go home, my father will say something like, 'Son, when are you going to get a real job and settle down and make some good money? You know you can always come to work for me.' I keep telling him 'Look, Dad, it's my life,' but I never tell him I'll be retiring from teaching college in two years."

Another good place to see regression in action is at the grocery store. I once witnessed an exchange between a mother in her mid-thirties and her daughter who must have been three or four. The mother, who looked exhausted and fried, was pushing the cart through the aisle; her daughter was in the seat looking at her. The little girl put her fingers in her ears and wagged them, then stuck out her tongue and said to her mother, "I'm mad at you and I'm not going to talk to you anymore!" Within a nanosecond the mother had her fingers in her own ears and with her tongue stuck out said, "Well I'm mad at you and I'm not going to talk to you anymore, either." The mother wasn't kidding. She was raging and regressing and demonstrating passivity par excellence. I thought, *Who is going to drive them home? They're both four, for goodness' sake.*

If your parents don't regress you, your children sure can.

Another and more recognizable way to think about regression is when a full-grown adult feels small or little. This happens when men and women feel like they've lost their age and maturity and feel six inches tall instead of six feet, or feel like a four-year-old instead of a forty-year-old.

Charles says, "Every time anyone looks at me in a certain way (which I can't even explain), I just want to scream at them, *What the hell are you looking at?* I think it's the way I felt when I had a real bad case of acne around fifteen or sixteen. I hated those years, but even more I hated the way people looked at me."

I have counseled many doctors, surgeons, and even nurses who have experienced rage and regression after losing a patient. When I asked them to describe their feelings, they all said almost exactly what the same thing—that they felt "little" or "small," as if they were frauds or actors playing a role they were not prepared for. This feeling comes to all of us no matter how powerful, successful, rich or poor, and it doesn't feel good.

Another way to recognize emotional regression is by the words many of us have said and heard—"I lost it!" or "I lost my temper."

Jamie said to me in a session, "Yesterday my husband, Todd, and I were having this very frank, honest, even refreshing conversation and I don't know what he said but I lost it. I started screaming at him all of a sudden and couldn't stop myself. He finally stormed out of the house and didn't come back for hours. What is that about? That wasn't my first temper tantrum, either."

"I found marijuana in my son's chest of drawers," said C.J. "And I don't know what happened but I lost it. When he came home from school, I yelled at him for two solid hours. I grilled him the way my father did when I was his age. We haven't spoken two words since. Here's the weird thing: I smoked grass at his age and swore if I ever caught my children doing it I'd approach it maturely, sanely, and rationally. But I was screaming my head off at him."

What do mature adults "lose" at these critical moments? The answer is many things, including logic, reason, rationality, maturity, and the ability to choose their words carefully and considerately. They lose their perspective, balance, and—most of all—their ability to stay in the prefrontal portion of their neocortex or new brain.

When people lose it, feel small, little, or less than the powerful person they are most of the time, and return to their pasts unintentionally, it can be explained not only emotionally but neurologically and biochemically as well.

THE BRAIN AND REGRESSION

The amygdala might be called the "little memory that keeps us safe" part of the brain. In other words, this almond-shaped segment of the brain remembers that thirty years ago someone in a black coat screamed at you and scared you to death. Thirty years later you see a man in a black coat coming toward you and you feel two inches tall and want to run and hide even though you don't know the man and he hasn't said a word.

When Ben was twelve, his math teacher spontaneously called on him to come to the front of the room and solve a problem on the chalkboard. What she didn't know—couldn't have known—was that Ben had a full erection from staring at Sharon Bennington all during the class. The teacher kept tapping the chalk on the board repeating his name over and over. "Every time she tapped that board and called my name my erection got bigger and bigger and I wanted to disappear. I finally went up there and everyone in the class saw it and laughed and to this very day if someone is tapping or calling my name in a certain way I become that twelve-year-old boy that was frustrated and full of rage at being singled out and embarrassed to death."

When we lose it, we leave the neocortex and head straight for the oldest part of the brain—the reptilian brain.

When we lose it, we leave the neocortex and head straight for the oldest part of the brain—the reptilian brain. This portion of the brain is only capable of notifying us when to eat, excrete, procreate, fight, take flight, or freeze—no logic, no reason, no choice, just the basic survival abilities.

Here's the key: When we regress, we go into fight mode—not with clubs like our ancestors, but with hard words and even harsher silence. Or we run away, fly away, drive away, and get the hell out of there. If we can't fly or fight, we freeze like the gazelle that can't outrun the faster cheetah. We passively freeze in dead marriages for thirty or forty years or dead-end jobs until retirement. We wait until the time has passed, the divorce is final, or the predator finds something else to chase. All of these are regressive reactions.

Emotional regression, then, is not a neurosis or psychosis. It can't be once and finally cured because it is simply a part of the human condition. However, we *can* identify and catch our regressions. This lets us come out of them and back into the present to our jobs, marriages, friendships, and families. The faster this happens, the better, since regressions usually equal regret. We are going to say something or not say something, do something or not do something while in a regressed state that we may regret for hours, days, or even decades. If we cannot make choices based on logic, reason, and ability to respond proportionately but only fight, fly from, or freeze out those we love, care about, or work with, the pain we create can sometimes be unbearable and too often unforgivable.

Emotional regression, then, is not a neurosis or psychosis. It is simply a part of the human condition.

Emotional Regression

A huge trigger for regression happens when we feel we are not being seen, really seen, for who we are, when we're being compared with someone in our past. "You're just like my first husband," "You are all alike," "All women lie," "All men cheat," "You're just like the other therapist." These phrases suggest what I call present-person people erasing; with them you replace the human being in front of you with someone from your past.

When Adrian and his wife, Lucy, argue, "She throws things. Her purse, pillows—nothing hard and she doesn't throw them at me, but it's like I see my father who did throw things at me when he was mad. He hurt me several times. I got a black eye once. I turn this five-foot-two, ninety-pound wife who wouldn't hurt a fly into a six-foot, two-hundred-pound dad from forty-some years ago." Adrian's regression caused Lucy to disappear and his father to come back out of the past—not a happy association.

Lonnie and Ramiro have been friends for twenty years. They've worked at the same farm equipment sales office as long as they've been friends.

"Two weeks ago I told Ramiro some personal stuff that I asked him to never tell any of the people we work with," Lonnie said, then paused and took a deep breath. "And that son-of-a-bitch blurted it out yesterday after work when a bunch of us met at a local bar. He'd had a few too many but I swear I want to kill him."

Lively Language

Lifeless language leads to a listless life. As unimaginative as that sentence is, it still beats, "When all is said and done." Passive people constantly speak in clichés that were worn out thirty years ago. The following phrases should have been laid to rest in a verbal cemetery somewhere a long time ago:

- *At the end of the day*
- *The perfect storm*
- *Slippery slope*
- *Opening the floodgates*
- *It's all good*
- *Rule of thumb*
- *Filthy rich*
- *Dirt poor*
- *Cold as ice*
- *Fresh as a daisy*
- *The best thing since sliced bread*

Long story short, Lonnie caught his regression and saw that his reaction was disproportionate. He realized he'd turned his close friend into not only an enemy, but his mother.

"When I was nine, I stole some eight-track tapes from a music store. I remember asking my mother not to tell my dad, who was out of town working. She promised she wouldn't and didn't for about two or three weeks. But one day she told him and he gave me the worst whipping of my life. I never trusted her again, and to be honest I've always had a hard time trusting people for fear they'll betray me ultimately. I realize I turned Ramiro into my mom, that he'd just made a simple mistake. I know when I bring it up he'll say he's sorry and we'll be fine."

When people's past is triggered, they tend to vent upon the one who triggered the emotional memory. Or they go to the least objectionable person possible.

When Jackie's husband left her, she said, "The first thing I did was call my mother, that's how regressed I was. My mother didn't finish calling him names before saying, 'I told you when I met Gary that he wasn't any good for you and that you could have done much better. Maybe you'll listen to your mother next time.' I felt about two years old. When she got through berating my husband—who by the way came back, and we eventually worked everything out—I was more enraged with her than when I was with him."

PART 4

WHAT NOW?

Midway on our life's journey, I found myself
In a dark woods, the right road lost. To tell
About those woods is hard—so tangled and rough . . .
　　　　　　　　　　　　—DANTE, *THE INFERNO*

The pivotal questions that must be answered, especially for those embarking on second half of their journey through this life, are:

- Where are you going?
- What are you going to do when you get there?
- Who are you going to do it with?
- What are you waiting for?

"Tell me, what is it you plan to do with your one wild and precious life?" asks the poet Mary Oliver. You may be thirty-five or sixty-five; we no longer know where the second half really starts. People are living so much longer, becoming so much healthier in mind, body, and spirit, that even the term *midlife* has become relatively meaningless. Still, the proverbial, perennial questions—"Is this really the life I want to lead?" or "Is this all there is?" or "What's it all about, Alfie?" (you have to be over fifty to get the last one)—must be answered.

WHERE ARE YOU GOING?

Let's start here. Where are you going? The prolific writer and former senior editor at *Psychology Today,* Sam Keen, said, "A man or woman must answer this question before asking 'Who is going to go with us?'"

Let's pretend that your family physician, God forbid, gave you some very disturbing news. You call me up in the middle of the night and say, "Help! John, my doctor says I only have seven years to live."

I say, "I am sorry to hear this bad news. Now let me ask you a question. Where are you going for those seven years?"

You may respond with the same scary answer that many have given me at forty or sixty when I've done this exercise in workshops: *"I don't know."*

Think about this question for a moment. Where do you want to go with the time that you have left? Do you want to stay in the same city? Same house? Do you want to sing along with David Byrne and the Talking Heads in their song "Same as It Ever Was" for those seven, seventeen, or seventy years you have left? You may, and that is quite an acceptable answer. But many would not stay where they are if they knew time was short. And it is.

I remember two friends of mine of forty years. Both had great jobs, money in the bank, wonderful retirement accounts. They loved the water, water sports, sand, and beaches and were dyed-in-the-wool "Parrot Heads" who followed Jimmy Buffett everywhere. I asked them what they were going to do when they retired. Without missing a beat they said they would go to the Florida Keys and open a little shop of some kind on the beach. I recall saying something like "Why don't you do that right now? You have plenty of money. You both are tired of your jobs and they don't give you any real joy." Burt answered for them both: "We can't just yet. We need a little more in our retirement fund. Beth will have full retirement benefits in two years and I will have them in four."

One year after that conversation Beth was diagnosed with lung cancer, having never smoked a day in her life. In a short six months, she was gone. No beach, no sand, no peaceful sanctuary but rather grief for all the missed opportunities.

Burt and Beth were not bad people. They were humble, hardworking, taxpaying citizens and great friends. They just never thought that "IT" would happen to them. You know what I'm talking about. We slow down to look at a car accident thinking it would never happen to us, and then speed up.

My own father yearned to be a lawyer and ended up a machinist who always thought he had plenty of time to quit and go back to school. He never did. Instead he drank most of his nights away until he was in his sixties. And while he is sober now (and has been for a long time), I always wonder: If he had been a lawyer, would he have needed to numb himself with such regularity? I remember saying to my father sometime in my late thirties how much I loved teaching college even though the pay was terrible. He said, "I can get you on at the plant making twice as much with overtime." When I responded, "Yeah, but I'd hate it. I love my job." He shot back, "What does love have to do with it? I never loved a day I went to work." I learned to look for the opposite.

My mom, who always wanted to be a preacher or a writer, ended up a fairly unhappy housewife projecting those deserted career choices onto guess who?

All right, if I haven't bummed you out sufficiently yet, let me tell you one more story about a man who didn't know where he wanted to go until he barely had enough time to find out and go there. Justin was, to repeat a theme, diagnosed with cancer and given six months to live. He came to see me for a two-day intensive, wanting to know how to make the most of the time he had left. We worked hard, and he remembered he had always wanted to visit the majestic redwood forest in California. He also had a beautiful fantasy of having all his children, grandchildren, wife, and closest friends to accompany him and lie down to make a circle around one of the smaller trees. When I asked him what had kept him from doing this earlier, the first word out of his mouth was "work." He went on to say that it would be too much of an imposition to get all those people to take off from their jobs, take on the travel expenses, and so forth. But now that he really did only have six months to live, he asked. And fourteen people went with him to the redwoods, circled that giant oak, stared with wonder at its magnificence, and surrendered their father/friend/husband to the same force that was responsible for growing it in the first place.

Are you ready to go back to the small town or big city that you left years ago, saying you would never go back in a million years? Are you ready to have a huge yard sale and sell everything but your flip-flops, Jet Ski, and Jimmy Buffett T-shirt and head for Margaritaville? Are you ready to make the old country singer Johnny Paycheck your true guru and tell your boss to "take this job and shove it"? Or perhaps you are quietly and calmly, with no fanfare or hoopla, headed to the one place that has always promised you peace, serenity, and purpose. If you are, hang on. I'm going to tell you something no one has ever told you that will make it much, much easier to do this. But first we have to answer the next question.

What Are You Going to Do When You Get There?

For some the answer to the question "What are you going to do with your seven years to live?" is "Play a lot of golf." There is absolutely nothing wrong with that answer. Some will say they are going to just "sit on the dock of the bay and watch the tide roll away." Good answer, to be sure. However, for most of us these answers aren't good enough. Most will answer, "I want to do what I wished I had done or always dreamed of doing."

If you tell me, "Look, I've paid my dues. I'm retired and I just want to live my life doing nothing," I will always say, "I hear you." But think about this for just a minute. Who was retirement originally meant for? It was for men and women who did menial, mind-numbing, backbreaking work. It was for people who stood in one place all day long pulling the same lever, inserting the same product in the same hole, getting maybe two weeks off a year and often not even that much. It was for those who worked overtime to pay the bills and never saw their families. It was for people who, for whatever reason, were taking a job rather than making their passions pay off.

The millions of us who came of age after World War II and received a college education tended to gravitate to work that forced us to use our brains instead of our brawn, our hearts instead of our hands. As this group stands on the border of what was and what will be, we still have fire in our bellies, energy in our bones, and a belief that we still have more to do, to contribute, to be, to help and heal. So is retirement really what most of us want to do with the twenty, perhaps even forty years left to us? I don't think so. Medical science and technology are now able to give us new hearts, lungs, livers, hips, knees, and so much more. We must find something to do that sets our souls ablaze.

A large number of men and women are working into their seventies, not so much because they love what they do but because, as they will often say, "I wouldn't know what to do with myself." In other words, they passively hang on to jobs that give their life some meaning and structure as well as income and purpose, rather than actively exploring what they would like to do should they leave the security their old jobs provide.

THE FIVE THINGS TO DO WHILE DISCOVERING YOUR AUTHENTIC SELF
Mentoring

Mentoring is a tradition that has withstood the test of time. This is because mentoring was and continues to be one of the most effective ways you can pass on the skills, knowledge, and wisdom you have acquired over the decades. If you ask a dozen different people what mentoring is, you will probably get at least a dozen different answers. Mentoring relationships can be informal and unstructured, more complex, or really casual. But what form they take is not as important as the learning that occurs and the kindness that is transferred between individuals. Everyone reading this right now would not have gotten where they are without some form of mentoring, even if it wasn't called that. Mentors do *Mentoring is a tradition that has withstood the test of time.* more than simply pass on knowledge and information; they pass on the most cherished parts of themselves and provide shortcuts learned via the hard knocks they received by doing things the harder way. As Ralph Waldo Emerson said, "Be an opener of doors for such as come after thee." An old Arabic proverb added, "A person starts out on a journey that takes him two hundred years to complete. If he had only had a good guide, it would have only taken two days."

Teaching

Teaching is one of the highest callings a man or woman can ever answer. It is a kissing cousin to mentoring, but with perhaps a bit more structure (though not always). A good friend of mine who is retired social worker understands the mysteries and machinations of money, investing, annuities, and other words I am not able to understand. He teaches me every time we talk on the phone as well as others in a way that is simple and down-to-earth. He believes in the old Chinese proverb, "Tell me and I'll forget; show me and I may remember; involve me and I'll understand."

As we all have heard, there are those who do and those who teach. Well, you have done and done again and now you really know what you know. So instead of thirty-six holes of golf on a sunny Saturday, play eighteen and set up a master class. Do it for free or for money, but pass on what you have learned in a way that will benefit others—and yourself.

Volunteering

Here is an excerpt from the book *Three Cups of Tea*, written by Greg Mortenson, one of my heroes of volunteerism: "If you really want to change a culture, to empower . . . improve basic hygiene and health care and fight high rates of infant mortality . . ." Greg was a mountain climber who became lost and ended up in a remote and impoverished Pakistani village. He was suffering from exposure, dehydration, and malnutrition. A Pakistani family took him in, treated him, and nursed him back to health. As Greg recovered, he thought long and hard about how he could best express his thanks to the villagers. The village elder and leader led him up a trail where children were scratching out letters with sticks in the dirt. The elder explained that this was the only school the children had. Right there and then Greg vowed that he would build a school for the village.

After many different kinds of struggles, Greg stayed true to his word and his vision and the school was constructed. It was the first of what would eventually become 130 schools built in remote areas of Pakistan and Afghanistan over the next sixteen years. Greg believes that the best way to attain peace is to volunteer and educate.

While most of us will never leave the comfort of our own hometown, we certainly must agree with Booker T. Washington: "If you want to lift yourself up, lift up someone else." And it was Margaret Mead who made clear, "Never doubt that a small group of committed people can change the world. Indeed, it is the only thing that ever has." It is never too late to volunteer, if not for the Peace Corps then for your own peace of mind.

Adopting

When most people hear the word *adopting* they think of babies no more than two or three years old. However, the majority of children waiting for parents are much older, and much forgotten.

I want to expand that thinking a little beyond children by suggesting other adoption programs—perhaps adopting a road that runs in front of your house that is often mistaken for a garbage dump and committing to picking up the trash that passive people throw out every day.

How about adopting a senior citizen who has little or no family to visit and bring news of the everyday world that is passing them by? We could become the people we see on the news occasionally who give their time and love to someone we may not even know well. There are also tens of thousands of dogs, cats, horses, and other creatures who are looking for kindness. Volunteer with your local vet or county animal shelter or take a furry or winged friend home with you at the end of the day.

Creating

I can't count the number of people I have worked with over the years who at some point around midlife decided the jobs they had been tethered to were meaningless and draining. I have seen bankers become bakers, writers become waiters, and salespeople become doctors—and they all found happiness and contentment, maybe not without some struggle and sacrifice, but they found the process worth it. Doing what you love is only part of the payoff. The process of making the decision and then following through is, for some, even more rewarding than the actual change of career. The willingness to go through the fears, overcome the passivity, go against traditional "wisdom" and engage the unknown makes life full and meaningful.

This great leap into the mystery is not only about what you end up doing but also about who you end up becoming, and the new friends, colleagues, and connections you make while pursuing your passion. You end up with a passionate life instead of a passive one.

In the beginning there was creativity. The cave paintings of Lascaux in France were done more than seventeen thousand years ago. Art found in South African caves suggests that we were creating at least seventy-seven thousand years ago.

Somewhere in there we stopped employing the imagination that was abundant in our youth and started letting a small group of others do it for us. In other words, we stopped listening to the call to create. Luckily for many that call is insistent, especially in the second half of life. By that point, we may have lain in bed too long staring out the window with longing. When we finally take the bright leap inside ourselves to actively participate in life, we're suddenly awash with ideas. By turning inward toward the creative impulses, we can begin to reclaim our lives. All our relationships take on a new fascination, a new sense of the unexpected, because people won't know what to expect from us—and we won't, either. That is the beauty and the promise implicit in the creative act.

Creativity is not reserved only for artists. It's for accountants, analysts, homemakers, bus drivers, executives, retirees, and members of any other vocation or avocation you can think of. Creativity can mean art in the traditional sense (visual arts, dance, theater, music, design . . .), but it can also mean projects, programs, inventions, education, and so much more.

By turning inward toward the creative impulses, we can begin to reclaim our lives.

When we were young, we were mystical thinkers, adventurers, poets, painters, pirates, cowboys, and Indians. But too soon we stopped creating castles with dragons and became rationalists too worried about credit ratings and stock portfolios to pursue our passions.

What creative endeavor is still calling with a whisper or a scream, showing up in your dreams, begging you to begin again?

WHO ARE YOU GOING WITH?

Now that you know (or at least are much closer to knowing) where you are going and what you are going to do, you can begin thinking about who you are going to include in this marvelous journey. When you think about having seven years ahead of you, you might include some people that would be excluded if you knew you only had seven months or seven weeks. As one workshop participant reflected, "If I have seven years, I would want my mother, father, sister, and two brothers to be included, and I would spend a significant amount of time with them. But if I only had seven months, I don't think I would spend very much time with them. With seven months or less, I would want to be with my husband and two daughters and the three women friends I've been close to for forty years. Is that wrong of me to not include my parents? I mean I love them, but . . ."

I responded, "No, it's not wrong. It is your seven months, not theirs. From what you have told me during this weekend, you were the primary caregiver in your family all during your childhood. This is your time, and any way you feel you need to spend it is right for you."

What Are You Waiting For?

So what are you waiting for? You can no longer blame lack of information and tools to work on your passivity, co-dependency, anger, or childhood traumas. It is time to stop waiting and dive into the next stage of life, like cliff divers certain the water below will be there when they arrive.

Perhaps you are waiting for your kids to grow up, your ship to come in, your divorce papers to be signed, and a severance check to be offered. Or maybe you are waiting for some kind of sign. You have probably been given enough of them already but up until now you denied or ignored them.

Are you waiting on a miracle to be performed in your honor? You are the miracle. You have participated in hundreds of miracles. All you have to do is remember them and let yourself open up to receive hundreds more. They are on the way.

Making a Miracle List

"America—It is a fabulous country, the only fabulous country; it is the only place where miracles not only happen, but where they happen all the time," says writer Tom Wolfe. He is talking about the same kind of miracles that I am in this section. One way to remind yourself of these is to make a miracle list.

This list consists of all the miracles in your life—big, small, medium, and gigantic, the things that happened to you, people who came into your life, jobs, friends, moves that you can look back on and say in all honesty were gifts, acts of grace. Yes, you have "free will," and yes you probably "showed up," but there was something about these miracles that you knew some greater thing, power, entity, or force had a hand in because you know you couldn't or wouldn't have made them happen on your best day.

Looking back on my sixty years, I can see miracles constantly moving in my direction. I remember the phone call that came at just the critical moment, the check that a loved one sent in the nick of time, the job, the one who came to teach me how to love. All of these things showed me that I do not have to rely on luck, attitude, positive thinking, or willpower, and certainly not on my innate intelligence. When I am not regressed, co-dependent, raging, afraid, and running away from people and things, I know with all my being there is a far greater intelligence that knows my needs way before I do. That intelligence is the greatest miracle of all.

As you prepare to make your leap into the unknown, remembering the miracles will further motivate you to trust and let go of what no longer works—or perhaps never really did. Making a list of miracles helps you go forward into the future with hope and confidence that you will be taken care of, shown the way, and be supported by others and the very universe to be who you have longed to be all your life, the one whom those who really know you know you could be. Making your own miracle list will demonstrate, as almost nothing can, compassion toward yourself and ultimately compassion toward everyone in your life. Because the more you are yourself, the more peace and serenity you will exude, and that will be the catalyst for them to pursue their own passions and dreams.

Anyone who doesn't believe in miracles isn't really paying attention. I'm not talking about miracles only as acts that go against natural laws (though I'm very open to these as well); I'm also referring to the simple, daily occurrences that are often blown off as coincidence or just plain luck. As you go into the next part of your life, remember the miracles in your past and count on them for your exciting future.

GOING INTO THE FUTURE WITH GRATITUDE

Gratitude is like a booster rocket to propel you even farther toward your discovery of your authentic self. It speeds you through the wildest ride of them all—actually doing what you really love.

May I suggest every morning or every evening making a short gratitude list, for one whole year—or longer. I did it for four years. It changed my life, and it will change yours and even those of the people around you.

The mystic philosopher Meister Eckhart said, "If the only prayer you said in your whole life was, 'thank you,' that would suffice." So as you think about the first half of your life, may I encourage you to thank yourself, your family, friends, teachers, enemies, children, jobs, loves, deaths, and whatever you consider to be higher and deeper than yourself—the Divine, God, your Higher Power, Spirit, whatever you call it.

Gratitude is the grand creator of grace, and this invisible, intangible something is what brought you to where you are. It will take you where you need to go so that you can do what you love. Gratitude is a door that leads to another door that leads to still more doors that are waiting to be opened and walked through.

I want to express my gratitude to you the reader for sticking with me and helping to make possible my own journey into the mysterious unknown. At the very back of this book, I will share in-depth my gratitude to specific people who have made me able to do what I love.

CONCLUSION

BEING WHO YOU REALLY ARE

You have traveled a long way with me, and now we come full circle. It is time to remind you of the definition of *passivity:* the compulsion to pursue the opposite of what we say we want. You have a variety of different and useful tools to help you come out of passivity and move into an active life fully prepared to be who you really are.

I will add one more thing that will clinch the deal. You may recall that in the introduction I mentioned the concept of false self. It is this constructed, compensatory self that saved your sanity, if not your life. The false self, also called our persona (which is the Greek word for "mask"), allowed you to negotiate the first part of your life, though not without some losses, pain, a few broken hearts, and many broken promises. It protected you and me the best it knew how. It was the one who became the captain of the football team when he longed to be in glee club, the hero who just wanted to follow, the peacekeeper who wished she could raise hell, the class clown who wanted to be a track star, the chairman of the board who was extremely bored, the dutiful son and daughter who dreamed of chaotic rebellion. It was this same false self who became the workaholic, addict, abuser, criminal, complainer, victim, co-dependent, and raging person. It was this one who was tirelessly chasing after money, power, prestige, value, appreciation, and validation from people who were not capable of giving it.

It is this false self who wants, wishes, dreams, and lives in a fantasy world. But now is the time to listen to the true self who whispers, "I don't really want this." As St. Paul says in Romans, "I do not understand what I do. For what I want to do I do not do . . ." One of my favorite Spanish poets, Juan Ramon Jimenez, comments on this separation very eloquently:

> *I am not I.*
> *I am this one*
> *walking beside me whom I do not see,*
> *whom at times I manage to visit,*
> *and whom at other times I forget;*
> *the one who remains silent while I talk,*
> *the one who forgives, sweet, when I hate,*
> *the one who takes a walk when I am indoors,*
> *the one who will remain standing when I die.*
> *—ENGLISH TRANSLATION BY ROBERT BLY*

It is the real self that is constantly dissatisfied with nearly all the things the false self achieves or acquires. The false self says, "I want power." The true self says, "I want peace." The pseudo-self says, "I want more and more and more money." The authentic self says, "Less is more." It is this true self that is forever seeking a way to show itself. Very often after a catastrophic event, a major personal loss, a sickness, death, or divorce, the true self shows up for a short time—only to be silenced after the crisis is over and the false self gets back to business as usual.

In order to come out of passivity and the implicit pain it constantly presents, we have to separate the false self from the real, hopefully without the catalyst of some near-death or great loss experience. In other words, we go gently into the time we have left, having had enough losses to last a lifetime or two.

Great spiritual teachers, poets, philosophers, and dreamers have been dropping bread crumbs for centuries that if followed will lead us to build a new, efficient home on solid rock instead of residing in the one a young man or woman built on shifting sand.

While I can't put myself in the company of the above-mentioned great guides, I can drop a few hints of my own on how to participate in this great divorce proceeding where the false self is occasionally realized and released and the true self is a free person to unite with whatever feels right.

The true or real self that you and I are and always have been will now be seen more and more often as it allows the next chapter of our lives to unfold a good deal more gracefully than the first. By being receptive and letting some magnificent intelligence drive the bus, we can count on a safe, satisfying,

The False Self	The True Self
• *Forces things to happen*	• *Lets things happen*
• *Tries to attract*	• *Magnetically attracts*
• *Pushes and pulls*	• *Rests*
• *Strains and stretches*	• *Relaxes and receives*
• *Fights and fumes*	• *Turns the other cheek and has fun*
• *Lies and embellishes*	• *Tells the truth at all costs*
• *Puts on airs*	• *Takes full deep breaths*
• *Resists aging*	• *Ages gracefully*
• *Rages*	• *Expresses anger appropriately*
• *Is full of self-pity*	
• *Holds on to everything*	• *Grieves all losses and changes*
• *Acquires creative things and people*	• *Lets go of everything*
• *Runs toward or away from*	• *Is the wellspring of creativity*
	• *Allows things to seek you*

sensational arrival. We no longer have to visualize, affirm, try, work, or even pray for our life to become what we really want, because the real self is accepting of where we are and knows where we need to go, what we need to do, and whom we are to take with us. It is not waiting on anything except our ever-increasing ability to trust in it.

The journey we are choosing to take must be first an emotional one, and what we have been taught is that we must take action first. Most of what we were told by well-intentioned people was taught by false selves. When we hear a true self speak—Jesus, Buddha, and living women and men masters—their words ring true in some part of us that is often referred to as soul, heart, or spirit.

The true self is synchronized with something eternal, something all-knowing, and when we are living from this place coincidences pop up mysteriously. Our life circumstances start changing, doors open, money comes, people are sent, and all we have to do is surrender our passive, false selves.

Unfortunately many people reading this think that surrender equals giving up or that it is a form of weakness or loss of power. Giving up is what passive people do every day. Surrendering engages every part of ourselves—the body, the spirit, the emotions, and the intellect. It is one of the most active things we can do when it is called for. It takes all our resources to force us out of the denial and dead-end patterns that proceed to nowhere. Surrendering requires that our whole being let go of rigid thinking, old angers, stress, tension, and most of all passivity.

The kind of surrendering the wise ones are modeling for us would agree with the German poet Goethe: "Destiny grants us our wishes, but in its own way, in order to give us something beyond our wishes." He goes on to imply that surrender is the first step and that "Whatever you do, or dream you can, begin it. Boldness has genius and power and magic in it."

Whatever you think you can do or believe you can do, begin it. Action has magic, grace, and power in it.

At its core every good self-help tome, holy book, psychology text, personal growth workshop, therapy session, and sermon you have ever been exposed to is trying to teach you about letting go of the false self.

The surrendering I am speaking of here allows and prepares us to open up to new people, places, possibilities, projects, ideas, and most of all an abundance of energy. The poet William Blake says, "Energy is pure delight," and a truly authentic life is all about using energy to engage love, compassion, creativity, and heightened consciousness and awareness of ourselves and others. The true self has more than enough energy and enthusiasm to take us into the next chapter of our lives. Now what are you going to do with your "one wild and precious life"?

Writing Your Next Chapter

Now that you have all the information and tools necessary to come out of any residual passivity that has been troublesome to you, it is time to see the next stage of your life as a series of blank pages. You are the author, editor, and publisher of your life. I encourage you to buy a very nice, leather-bound journal and fill the pages with your thoughts, feelings, insights, fears, and fantasies about the exciting future that awaits you now that you are no longer waiting on it. Or use a cheap notebook, or your computer screen. You are worth the time.

ACKNOWLEDGMENTS

I always tell new writers to look at the acknowledgments page to find out what authors say about their agent. Here's what I have to say about Penny Nelson at Manus Literary Agency. She does not display any passivity at all when it comes to working tirelessly on behalf of those she represents. Were it not for her strong belief and dedication to this project, it would not have been written or published—thank you so much, Penny, for your continued belief in me and my work.

I want to express my deep gratitude for my editor Mary Norris at Lyons Press for her talents and great temperament. She is a writer's dream editor—thanks so much for your patience and exuberance.

Also many thanks go to Kristen Mellitt for her careful and creative editing skills and talents.

My heartfelt thanks to my wife, Susan Lee, a confidante, friend, and really good writer and editor. I hope you know by now how much I appreciate your love and support and trust your judgment.

There is a whole host of folks who keep me going when I'm all but ready to throw in the proverbial towel—I hope by now you know who you are but just in case—Robert Bly, Bill Stott, Dr. James Maynard, my sister Kathy McClelland, Karen Blicher, Connie Burns, Terry Allen, Pat Love, Tony Goggans, Bill Rutledge, Roger Fuller, Bob White, Dane Dixon, all the PEER folks.

Blessings on you all.

Index

ABOUT THE AUTHOR

 John Lee's highly innovative work in the fields of emotional intelligence, passivity, anger management, and emotional regression has made him an in-demand consultant, teacher, trainer, coach, and speaker. His contributions in the fields of recovery, relationships, men's issues, spirituality, parenting, and creativity have put him in the national spotlight for more than twenty years.

He has been featured on *Oprah, Dr. Oz, 20/20,* Barbara Walters's *The View,* CNN, PBS, and NPR. He has been interviewed by *Newsweek,* the *New York Times,* the *Los Angeles Times,* and dozens of other national magazines and radio talk shows.

John Lee has consulted and trained at prestigious institutions in the clinical environment, including the Cleveland Clinic, the Betty Ford Clinic, Guy's Hospital (London, England), the New York Open Center, South Pacific Private Hospital (Sydney, Australia), Mountain Area Health and Education Center (North Carolina), and numerous others.

His unique approach to anger management has been embraced not only by the therapeutic community but by the corporate sector and the general public as well. His nontraditional approach to therapy has been taught world-wide with great success. His two-day Mentone intensives have attracted highly motivated clients who want more one-on-one time than the usual fifty-minute hour can provide.

John's work with men's issues has positioned him as one of the leaders and early pioneers of the men's movement. His Mentone, Alabama, Men's Conference (co-hosted with Robert Bly) is in its sixteenth year and draws participants from around the world.

Over the past two decades, John Lee has conducted private and group sessions on a variety of issues working with men, women, couples, and families. He lectures, gives workshops, and conducts training in more than forty cities each year, delivering sensitive, sophisticated material to audiences in a humorous and simple way everyone can understand. His lectures have been branded as "hilariously entertaining, deeply compassionate, yet filled with 'tell it like it is!'"

John served as a professor at the University of Texas and the University of Alabama before becoming a writer, best-selling author, life coach, and personal consultant. He lives with his wife in Alabama and Texas.

To contact John Lee for speaking engagements, consulting, one-on-one two- and three-day intensives, or phone sessions, or to order CDs, go to www.johnleebooks.com or call (678) 494-1296.